SWU-800- 013

# UNIFORMS OF RUSSIAN ARMY DURING THE YEARS 1825-1855 VOL. 13

## UNDER THE REIGN OF NICHOLAS I
### EMPEROR OF RUSSIA BETWEEN 1825 TO 1855
#### IRREGULAR TROOPS, FLAGS & OTHERS - PART 1

From the Viskovatov's greatest work:
"Historical description of the clothing and
arms of the Russian Army"

English translation by Mark Conrad

# SOLDIERSHOP PUBLISHING

## AUTHOR

Aleksandr Vasilevich Viskovatov born 22 April (4 May New Style) 1804, died 27 February (11 March) 1858 in St. Petersburg, Russian military historian. He graduated from the 1st Cadet Corps and served in the artillery, the hydrographic depot of the Naval Ministry, and then in the Department of Military Educational Institutions. He mainly studied historical artifacts and the histories of military units. Viskovatov's greatest work was the Historical Description of the Clothing and Arms of the Russian Army.

Title: **UNIFORMS OF RUSSIAN ARMY DURING THE YEARS 1825-1855. VOL. 13** -Under the reign of Nicholas I emperor of Russia between 1825-1855

By A.V.Viskovatov. Serie edit by Luca S. Cristini. First edition by Soldiershop. July 2019

Cover & Art Design: Luca S. Cristini. Plates re-colorations by Anna Cristini. ISBN code: 978-88-93274302

Published by Luca Cristini Editore, via Orio 35/4- 24050 Zanica (BG) ITALY. www.soldiershop.com

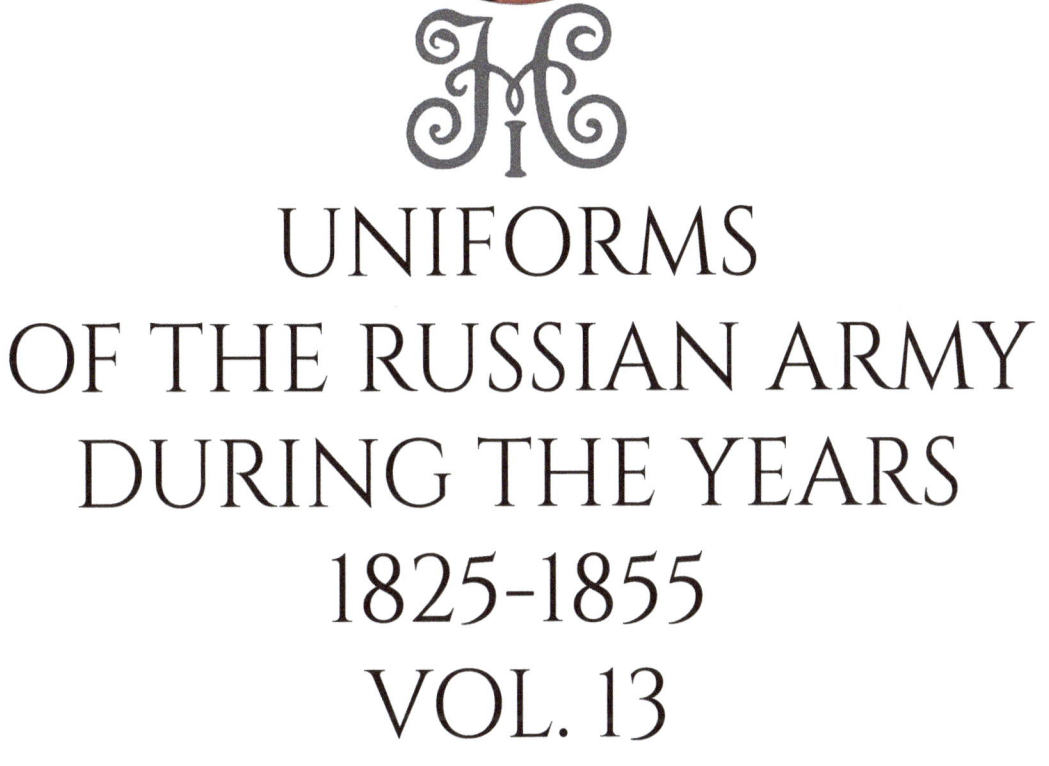

# UNIFORMS
# OF THE RUSSIAN ARMY
# DURING THE YEARS
# 1825-1855
# VOL. 13

UNDER THE REIGN OF NICHOLAS I  EMPEROUR OF
RUSSIA BETWEEN 1825 AND 1855

*

IRREGULAR TROOPS, FLAGS & OTHERS - PART. 1

*Portrait of an officer of irregular cossacks*

# HISTORICAL DESCRIPTION OF THE CLOTHING AND ARMS
## OF THE RUSSIAN ARMY - A.V. VISKOVATOV
### (First English translation by Mark Conrad)

Soldiershop is glad to presents the complete collection of the great job made by A.V. Viskovatov dedicated to the uniforms and weapons belonging from the first Zar and Russian emperors to the Russian army during the Napoleonic period, until 1860 about. The time we considered in this volume corresponds to the reigns of Nicholas I that was the Emperor of Russia from 1825 until 1855. He was also the King of Poland and Grand Duke of Finland. He is best known as a political conservative whose reign was marked by geographical expansion, repression of dissent, economic stagnation, poor administrative policies, a corrupt bureaucracy, and frequent wars that culminated in Russia's defeat in the Crimean War of 1853–56.

Our reprint in based on the original 19th century volumes. This part is distributed at now on six volumes.

Our new edition, the first ever published in English, both on paper and digital format, boasts a large number of color plates, many of them unpublished and re-coloured by our team of expert artists and scholars of uniformology. Each volume is based on 100 color plates or more, always accompanied by the original translated text which describes the subjets of the plates.

A unique work in its genre, a must have in any respecting collection!

Aleksandr Vasilevich Viskovatov born 22 April (4 May New Style) 1804, died 27 February (11 March) 1858 in St. Petersburg, Russian military historian. He graduated from the 1st Cadet Corps and served in the artillery, the hydrographic depot of the Naval Ministry, and then in the Department of Military Educational Institutions.

He mainly studied historical artifacts and the histories of military units. Viskovatov's greatest work was the Historical Description of the Clothing and Arms of the Russian Army (Vols. 1-30, St. Petersburg, 1841-62; 2nd ed. Vols. 1-34, St. Petersburg - Novosibirsk - Leningrad, 1899-1948). This work is based on a great quantity of archival documents and contains four thousand colored illustrations.

Viskovatov was the author of Chronicles of the Russian Army (Books 1-20, St. Petersburg, 1834-42) and Chronicles of the Russian Imperial Army (Parts 1-7, St. Petersburg, 1852). He collected valuable material on the history of the Russian navy which went into A Short Overview of Russian Naval Campaigns and General Voyages to the End of the XVII Century (St. Petersburg, 1864; 2nd edition Moscow, 1946). Together with A.I. Mikhailovskii-Danilevskii he helped prepare and create the Military Gallery in the Winter Palace.

He wrote the historical military inscriptions for the walls of the Hall of St. George in the Great Palace of the Kremlin. (From the article in the Soviet Military Encyclopedia.)

# CONTENTS

\*

# HISTORICAL DESCRIPTION OF THE CLOTHING AND ARMS OF THE RUSSIAN ARMY

## Irregular Troops, Temporary Forces, Flags, Orders, and Medals 1825-1855 part 1

### Chapter LXXX
### III. THE CAUCASIAN LINE COSSACK HOST. [*KAVKAZSKOE LINEINOE KAZACHE VOISKO.*]
REGIMENTS

**1 January 1827** - In order to differentiate between **ranks**, small stamped stars [*kovanye zvezdochki*] are established for officers' epaulettes, as for regular forces (1).

**7 August 1829** - **Epaulettes** on officers' uniforms are to have scaled fields [*cheshuichatoe pole*] like the pattern of epaulettes in the regular light cavalry (2).

**16 January 1831** - For regiments of the **Caucasian Line Cossack Host** without prescribed uniforms, there are introduced: half-caftan, or *cherkeska*, as an outer garment [*verkhnee polukaftan'e ili cherkska*], without collar or cuffs, trimmed around with black tape, with two cartridge-holders on the breast [*nagrudnye patronniki*] of green morocco leather, and two sholder straps; a caftan, or *beshmet*, worn underneath [*nizhnii kaftan ili beshmet*]; narrow pants; headdress with a round cloth crown with a wide brim of black sheep's fleece; narrow leather belt; shashka or saber [*shashka ili sablya*] in a black leather scabbard, dagger, musket, and pistol. Officers are prescribed the same uniform but with narrow silver galloon instead of tape and with silver scaled epaulettes, which are allowed not to be worn when in operations against the enemy.

Uniform colors are designated as follows: In the **Terek Family Regiment**—very dark-blue [*temnosinii*] *cherkesa* and pants, red *beshmet* and headdress, red shoulders straps with the No. 1 (Illus. 1194). In the **Khoper Regiment**—very dark-blue *cherkeska* and pants, white *beshmet* and headdress, white shoulder straps with the No. 1 (Illus. 1194). In the **Mountaineer Regiment**—very dark-blue *cherkeska* and pants, yellow *beshmet* and headdress, sky-blue shoulder straps with the No. 1 (Illus. 1195). In the **Grebensk Regiment**—very dark-blue *cherkeska* and pants, sky-blue [*goluboi*] *beshmet* and headdress, sky-blue shoulder straps with the No. 1 (Illus. 1195). In The **Kuban Regiment**—dark-brown [*temnokorichnevyi*] *cherkeska* and pants, red *beshmet* and headdress, red shoulder straps with the No. 2 (Illus. 1196). In the Volga Regiment—dark-brown *cherkeska* and pants, white *beshmet* and headdress, white shoulder straps with the No. 2 (Illus. 1196). In the **Mozdok Regiment**—dark-brown *cherkeska* and pants, yellow *beshmet* and headdress, yellow shoulder straps with No. 2 (Illus. 1197). In the **Kizlyar-Terek Regiment**—dark-brown *cherkeska* and pants, sky-blue *beshmet* and headdress, sky-blue shoulder straps with the No. 2 (Illus. 1197) (3).

**April 1831** - **Officers without permanent positions** [*za-uryad-ofitsery*] are to have small forged and stamped stars on their epaulettes like those introduced on 1 January 1827 to distinguish rank (4).

**21 May 1834** - The following colors are prescribed for the uniforms of the **Caucasian Line Cossack Host**:

*Caucasian Regiment*—very dark-blue cherkeska and pants; beshmet and headdress red, red shoulder straps with the No. 1 in yellow (Illus. 1198).

*Kuban*—very dark-blue cherkeska and pants, white beshmet and headdress, white shoulder straps with the No. 1 in red (Illus. 1198).

*Stavropol*—very dark-blue cherkeska and pants, yellow beshmet and headdress, yellow shoulder straps with the No. 1 in red (Illus. 1199).

*Khoper*—very dark-blue cherkeska and pants, light-blue [*svetlosinii*] beshmet and headdress, light-blue shoulder straps with the No. 1 in red (Illus. 1199).

*Volga*—very dark-blue cherkeska and pants, light-green beshmet and headdress, light-green shoulder straps with No. 1 in red (Illus. 1200).

*Mountaineer*—dark-brown cherkeska and pants, red beshmet and headdress, red shoulder straps with the No. 2 in yellow (Illus. 1200).

*Mozdok*—dark-brown cherkeska and pants, white beshmet and headdress, white shoulder straps with No. 2 in red (Illus. 1201).

*Grebensk*—dark-brown cherkeska and pants, yellow beshmet and headdress, yellow shoulder straps with the No. 2 in red (Illus. 1201).

*Terek*—dark-brown cherkeska and pants, light-blue beshmet and headdress, light-blue shoulder straps with the No. 2 in red (Illus. 1202).

*Kizlyar*—dark-brown cherkeska and pants, light-green beshmet and headdress, light-green shoulder straps with No. 2 in red (Illus. 1202). It is ordered that officers' uniforms be distinguished from lower ranks' by silver galloon and silver scaled epaulettes lined with red cloth; the headdress has silver galloon with a black brim (5).

**28 July 1836** - The **Kizlyar Family Regiment** [*Semeinyi-Kizlyarskii polk*], formed from the Terek and Kizlyar Cossack Regiments, is prescribed the uniform of the former Terek Regiment (6).

**8 April 1843** - In the Caucasian Line Cossack Host it is ordered that *officers' greatcoats* have standing collars of the color prescribed for the collar of the arkhaluk in each regiment; buttons are white (Illus. 1203) (7).

**2 October 1843** - The **Laba and Vladikavkaz Cossack Regiments** are prescribed uniforms: Laba—of dark blue [*sinii*] with an orange arkhaluk; shoulder straps and top of the headdress of the same color (Illus. 1204). Vladikavkaz—of brown with a green arkhaluk; shoulder straps and headdress top of the same color (Illus. 1204) (8).

**14 February 1843** - By a confirmed Regulation the regiments of the **Caucasian Line Cossack Host** are prescribed the following uniforms, weapons, and horse furniture.

### 1st and 2nd Caucasian Regiments.

### For cossacks.

Half-round headdress, the top (*bashlyk*) of red cloth, the brim of shaggy black kurnei, chinstrap of black silk tape. Coat (*cherkeska*) of dark-blue cloth, without collar or cuffs, reaching to 2 vershoks [3-1/2 inches] below the knees, closed by small hooks from the cartridge-holders to the belt. Red beshmet for the coat, stamin, 1 vershok [1-3/4 inches] shorter than the coat. Black cartridge-holders on the coat, of leather, with inside pockets lined with black lace and black cord; birch tubes [*vtulki berezovye*] with white bone caps. Each cartridge-holder holds 8 cartridges. Red shoulder straps, of cloth with the punched-out designation of the regiment: 1 K (first Caucasian), 2 K (second Caucasian). Dark-blue cloth pants with small leather straps at the feet. Red woollen pistol lanyard. Cloth pistol holder, the upper part red and the lower dark blue. In place of a greatcoat—a Caucasian *burka* [fur cape - M. C.]. Girdle—a black strap 1/2 vershok [7/8 inch] wide with a grease box [*zhirnitsa*] and strap for the dagger; iron fittings. Sword belt—Circassian, a black leather strap with iron fittings.

Pistol—Circassian, of any desired pattern. Sword—Circassian shashka, of the pattern for troops in the Caucasus. Circassian dagger, decorated as desired. Circassian musket, of no established pattern. Musket case—of leather, trimmed outside with wool. Cartridge pouch [*patrontash*]—of black leather, for 20 cartridges in a single row; instead of a cross strap for the pouch a black silk ribbon 1/4 vershok [1/2 inch] wide is used. Powder holder—horn, with smooth metal mountings. To this there is to be a cord similar to that for the pistol.

The saddle consists of a tree, girth, stirrup straps with stirrups, saddle cloth, crupper, and surcingle with pad. Valise and pillow are of black leather trimmed around the edges with red morocco. The bridle is of rawhide with iron fittings. Halter made from rawhide straps. Circassian nagaika whip (Illus. 1205).

For non-commissioned officers [*uryadniki*]. Headdress the same as for cossacks but the top lined with silver galloon. Coat the same as for cossacks but with silver galloon sewn around the neck opening down to the waist and along the lower edges of the sleeves. Silver galloon trim on the beshmet along the collar and front opening to the waist. Cartridge-holders, shoulder straps, sharovary pants, and all other parts of the uniform and weaponry are as for cossacks.

Officers.

The same beshmet as for lower ranks but instead of red stamin—red shalloon [*shalonovyi*]. Cartridge-holders (for 8 cartridge each) are black velvet with inside pockets, trimmed around with wide silver lace; tubes of Karelian birch with silvered caps. Silver epaulettes, scaled, with the same field, on which—as on the buttons—is the regimental sign. Sharovary pants—of the pattern for lower ranks but with two rows of silver galloon down the side seams. Cord—for the pistol, silver. Holder—for the pistol, the same as for lower ranks but trimmed along the seams with silver galloon. Girdle of black lace, interwoven with silver, 1/2 vershoks [7/8 inch] wide, with a grease box and strap for the dagger; fittings silver with black. Sword belt as for lower ranks but with silvered mountings. Shashka sword with a silver sword knot. Valise and saddle pad trimmed around the edges with silver galloon in addition to red morocco. Bridle with silvered fittings.

Headdress, coat, burka, pistol, dagger, saddle with valise and pad, halter, and nagaika whip—in all respects similar to those prescribed for lower ranks.

The lace and galloon for uniforms in the host are to be of Asiastic manufacture throughout, this product being known for its durability and low coast.

The *1st and 2nd Kuban Regiments* are to have all the above items as for the 1st and 2nd Caucasian Regiments, but the head-dress, beshmet, shoulders straps, pistol lanyard, and upper part of the pistol holder are white (Illus. 1206).

*1st and 2nd Laba Regiments*—as for the above regiments, but orange headdress, beshmet, shoulder straps, pistol lanyard, and upper part of the pistol holder; on the shoulder straps the regiment's marking: 1 L in Cyrillic (first Laba), and 2 L (second Laba) (Illus. 1206).

*1st and 2nd Stavropol Regiments*—as for the above regiments, but green headdress, beshmet, shoulder straps, pistol lanyard, and upper part of the pistol holder; on the shoulder straps the regiment's marking: 1 S in Cyrillic (first Stavropol), and 2 S (second Stavropol) (Illus. 1207).

*1st and 2nd Khoper Regiments*—as for the above regiments, but yellow headdress, beshmet, shoulder straps, pistol lanyard, and upper part of the pistol holder; on the shoulder straps the regiment's marking: 1 Kh in Cyrillic (first Khoper), and 2 Kh (second Khoper) (Illus. 1207).

*1st and 2nd Volga Regiments*—as for the above regiments, but light-blue headdress, beshmet, shoulder straps, pistol lanyard, and upper part of the pistol holder; on the shoulder straps the regiment's marking: 1 V in Cyrillic (first Volga), and 2 V (second Volga) (Illus. 1208).

*Mountaineer Regiment*—as for the Caucasian regiments, but brown coat, sharovary pants, and lower part of the pistol holder; on the shoulder straps the Cyrillic letter G (*Gorskii*) (Illus. 1208).

*Mozdok Regiment*—as for the Kuban regiments, but brown coat, sharovary pants, and lower part of the pistol holder; on the shoulder straps the Cyrillic letter M (Mozdok) (Illus. 1209).

*Grebensk Regiment*—as for the Khoper regiments, but brown coat, sharovary pants, and lower part of the pistol holder; on the shoulder straps the Cyrillic letters Gr (Grebensk) (Illus. 1209).

*Vladikavkaz Regiment*—as for the Stavropol regiments, but brown coat, sharovary pants, and lower part of the pistol holder; on the shoulder straps the Cyrillic letter V (Vladikavkaz) (Illus. 1210).

*Kizlyar Family Regiment*—as for the Volga regiments, but brown coat, sharovary pants, and lower part of the pistol holder; on the shoulder straps the Cyrillic letter K (Kizlyar) (Illus. 1210) (9).

**19 March 1847** - The **1st Sunzha Cossack Regiment** is ordered to have the following uniform clothing: coat and sharovary pants of brown, of the patterns for other regiments of the Caucasian Line Cossack Host; orange beshmet, top to the headdress, and cords, following the example of the Laba regiments; cloth shoulder straps of the same color, with the Cyrillic letters 1 C. punched out [*vybitye*] on them, signifying the 1st Sunzha Regiment; arms and horse furniture (Illus. 1211) according to the description appended to the Host Regulation (Appendix IX). The exact same uniform is ordered for the 2nd Sunzha Regiment whenever it may be formed (10).

**13 February 1849** - The following uniform and weaponry are confirmed for the **1st Caucasian Cossack Foot Battalion** (Illus. 1212).

**Officers**.

Headdress—cloth dark-green top, trimmed in the center with 4 rows of Circassian galloon and in 1 row around the inside of the lambskin brim. Brim of black lamb's fleece; black chinstrap. Chekmen coat of dark-green cloth in the style of the Asiatic beshmet, with a rounded collar, but with cuffs as for Black Sea Cossack battalions. Red piping on the collar, down the front, and along the cuffs and pockets. The chekmen must be 5 vershoks [8-3/4 inches] above the knees. Dark-green cloth sharovary pants, with a drawstring, no stripes. Cartridge-holders on the chest of black cloth trimmed with Circassian galloon after the fashion for horse regiments; 16 cartridges mounted in silver.

Circassian dagger mounted in silver. Black silk cord. Circassian shashka sword, mounted in silver. Pistol holder—black cloth with piping the same color as the shoulder straps on the ends and middle. Pistol carrier—black morocco; instead of piping—Circassian galloon; worn at the back on the belt.

Waistbelt of black tape with silver edging, lined with black morocco, with silver small and large buckles, slide, and tip. Sword belt of the same tape as the waistbelt, with silver fittings, also lined with black morocco. Sword knot of the usual infantry pattern. Silver epaulettes with cloth the same color as for the headdresses in horse regiments, with the gold embroidered number and letter 1 K; backed with black cloth.

Greatcoat of grey army cloth with a black collar and tab the same color as the headdress in horse regiments, with a silver button and the characters 1 K. The collar is also lined with black cloth.

**Cossacks.**

Headdress the same as for officers; for non-commissioned officers trimmed with Circassian galloon crossing in two rows. Chekmen the same as for officers, except for non-commissioned officers the collar and cuffs are trimmed with Circassian galloon. Dark-green sharovary pants, with drawstring, no stripes. Cartridge-holders on the chest—of black morocco trimmed with black tape; 12 cartridges in ivory. Dagger with a bone handle; bayonet in scabbard. Black waistbelt of Circassian leatherwork, with cast iron fittings. Shoulder straps the same color as the headdress in horse regiments with the punched out characters 1 K, backed with yellow cloth. Cartridge-holders for 28 cartridges, of the pattern for Black Sea Cossack foot battalions. Greatcoat of army soldier cloth with the same collar, tabs, and shoulder straps with the characters 1 K, as for officers; tin buttons with the same characters. The greatcoat is to be carried rolled in the infantry manner. Knapsack of black Russian leather, with black straps, of the pattern for the Separate Caucasus Corps.

Drummers: the same headdress as for officers except trimmed with white tape in two rows crosswise and in one row around the lambskin. Chekmen the same as for officers except that the collar, front opening, cuffs, and pockets are trimmed with two rows of white tape; epaulettes of the pattern for Army drummers with piping the same colors as the shoulder straps. Sharovary pants and cartridge-holders on the breast, as for cossacks. Dagger with bone handle. Pistol after the Circassian fashion. Black woollen cord. Pistol holder the same as for officers. Pistol carrier of black morocco without galloon. Waistbelt, shoulder straps, greatcoat, and knapsack as for cossack (11).

**7 May 1849** - In the uniform for officers of the **1st Caucasian Cossack Foot Battalion** as established on 13 February 1849, it is ordered to make the following changes: the galloon used to trim the headdress, cartridge-holders, and pistol carrier is to be that used in the Caucasian Line Cossack Host. Silver pistol lanyard. Girdle and sword belt to be made from black silk tape with silver stripes along the edges; the stripes are to have a toothed pattern and a gold light. On the epaulettes the characters 1 K are to be made from silver thread the same color as the epaulette tinsel [*epoletnaya mishura*]; under the epaulettes the cloth is to be red. Instead of 8 cartridges fitting awkwardly on the breast of the chekmen, there are to be only 6 on each side; the cartridges themselves are to be held by fine silver chains; the red piping in the back on the chekmen pockets is abolished; red piping on the sharovary pants (Illus. 1212) (12).

**12 February 1851** - In regard to uniforms and arms for **generals, staff duty officers, adjutants for special assignments, aides to adjutants**, and personnel serving in the Caucasian Line Cossack Host's **internal administration**, the following changes are ordered.

Headdress (*papakha*) of the pattern confirmed for the Separate Caucasus Corps: for generals wearing the standard general officer's parade half-caftan, the top of the headdress is to be of red cloth with gold general officer's embroidery along the four seams and lower edge; for staff duty officers, adjutants for special assignments, aides to adjutants, and officers serving in the internal administration—the top of the headdress is to be of dark-green cloth with silver galloon, with two narrow red stripes down the galloon's middle.

Undress half-caftan [*vitsepolukaftan*] for all these personnel except generals. The undress half-caftan is the same cut as the parade but without buttonhole loops on the collar and without flaps on the cuffs. Girdles are not prescribed for wear with the undress half-caftan.

Weapons: for generals wearing the standard general officer's parade half-caftan, a dragoon saber instead of a cavalry saber, of the pattern confirmed for the Separate Caucasus Corps, worn on a sword belt over the shoulder made from gold galloon and lined with black morocco. Swordbelt fittings are gilt. When wearing Host uniform, however, a *shashka* sword as prescribed for the Host, on the sword belt of the confirmed pattern. For staff duty officers, adjutants for special assignments, aides to adjutants, and officers serving in the internal administration—instead of a cavalry saber, the *shashka* as prescribed for the Host, worn over the shoulder on a sword belt of silver galloon backed with black morocco. Silver fittings for this sword belt (13).

**16 December 1851** - The following uniforms and arms are confirmed for the **Daghestan Irregular Horse Regiment** (Illus. 1213).

**For officers.**

Headdress—of the pattern for the Caucasian Line Cossack Host with a brim of black lamb's wool; top of red cloth; trimmed with 8 rows of silver galloon crosswise and one row around the brim.

*Chukha* (outer dress)—of the pattern for the coat in the Caucasian Line Cossack Host, of black factory-made European cloth; trimmed around the ends of the sleeves and along the side pockets with semi-wide silver galloon. The cartridge-holders [*rutsali* or *gozyri*] on the *chukha*—of red velvet for 20 cartridges; trimmed with 4 rows of silver galloon; the ends of the cartridges silvered. Green silk *arkhaluk* of Lezghin style; trimmed with narrow silver gallon: two rows on the collar, 1 row on the front opening and ends of the sleeves. Silver epaulettes and likewise shoulder straps. *Sharovary* pants of black cloth, sewn in Lezghin style, trimmed along the side seams and at the bottom edges with narrow silver galloon. Footwear is European boots. Girdle, straps and belts for the *shashka*—of silver galloon.

Circassian *shashka* sword in stamped silver mountings, with a silver hilt. Dagger in silver mountings with a white bone handle. Asiatic pistol in silver mountings, worn on a silver cord. Cartridge pouch of red morocco for 20 cartridges, trimmed with semi-narrow silver galloon. Silver grease-box [*sal'nitsa*]. Silver powderhorn for gunpowder.

Non-commissioned officers (*uryadniki*, or *vekili*), private horsemen, and clerks.

Headdress as for officers with a brim of black lambskin; cloth top for *vekili* and horsemen: 1st Sotnia - red, 2nd - green, 3rd - yellow, 4th - sky blue, 5th - white, 6th dark blue, for clerks - red.

*Chukha* of black Lezghin cloth, trimmed around the ends of the sleeve and along the side pockets with narrow silver galloon for *vekili* and clerks, and with narrow white tape for horsemen. Cartridge-holders of red cloth, for 20 cartridges; trimmed with 4 rows of narrow silver galloon for *vekili* and clerks, and black tape for horsemen; black bone ends to the cartridges in the holder. *Arkhaluk* of green *burmet* (Persian cotton cloth); for *vekili* and clerks trimmed with narrow silver galloon, and for horsemen with narrow white tape—in 2 rows around the collar, 1 row down the front and at the ends of the sleeves. *Sharovary* pants of dark-blue burmet, without any trimming. Plain native Lezghin footwear. Girdle, belts, and straps for the *shashka* are of black leather of Asiatic rawhide manufacture.

Circassian *shashka* sword in a leather scabbard, with a black bone handle. Dagger in a black leather sheath without any mountings, with a black bone handle. Asiatic musket, carried in a case of mountaineer style, on a black rawhide strap over the right shoulder. Clerks are not prescribed muskets. Asiatic pistol without any mountings, worn on a black tape ribbon. Cartridge pouch of red *mishina* (semi-morocco) of Asiatic manufacture, for 20 rounds, trimmed with black tape; not authorized for clerks. White tin grease-box. Black bone or horn powerhorn.

The uniforms and weapons described here make up officers' parade and summer campaign dress, and for winter campaign dress the *chukha* is lined with fur. For lower ranks the uniform described is the summer dress; for winter dress the *chukha* is lined with fur and the *sharovary*, instead of being dark-blue cotton, are made from black Lezghin cloth.

When on the march or on campaign native mountaineers in the Daghestan Regiment were noted wearing a wrap, or *tolakha*, covering the legs almost to the knees. In summer it was made of silk or cotton cloth, and in winter of thick felt [*voilok*] or woollen cloth. Dimensions of the clothing and weapons are as follows: *chukha* sleeves reach to the tips of the fingers and are 4 vershoks [7 inches] wide at the ends, with a slit reaching 4 vershoks from the end opening; the *chukha* skirts reach 2 vershoks [3-1/2 inches] below the knees. *Arkhaluka* collar—1 to 1-1/2 vershoks [1-3/4 to 2-5/8 inches] high; *arkhaluka* skirts reach to 2 vershoks [3-1/2 inches] above the knees; sleeves reach to the wrist, and its upper part, thrown forward, covers the hand with its semicircular end reaching to the tips of the fingers; *sharovary* pants covered all from the waist to the heels, its lower end being 4 to 4-1/2 vershoks [7 to 7-7/8 inches] wide.

Daggers for lower ranks are 3/4 to 1 arshin [21 to 28 inches] long, 1-1/4 to 1-1/2 vershoks [2-3/16 to 2-5/8 inches] wide; for officers a little smaller.

Noncombatant lower ranks in the regiment—apothecary apprentice, medical orderly, lazaret attendants, and barbers—have the same uniforms as for these ranks in regular regiments (14).

## ARTILLERY

**1 January 1827** - In order to distinguish **rank**, small stamped stars are established for officers' epaulettes, as in for regular troops (15).

**7 August 1829** - **Epaulettes** on officers' uniforms are ordered to have a scaled field as for the epaulette pattern for regular light cavalry (16).

**April 1831** - **Officers without permanent positions** [*za-uryad-ofitsery*] are to have small forged or stamped stars on their epaulettes like those introduced on 1 January 1827 to distinguish rank (17).

**14 February 1845** - By the Regulation for the Caucasian Line Cossack Host confirmed on this date, this host's horse-artillery batteries (13, 14, and 15) are prescribed **uniforms**, **weapons**, and **horse furniture** as follows.

### Cossacks.

Half-round headdresses, the top (*bashlyk*) of red cloth, brim of shaggy black lambskin, chinstrap of black silk tape. Coat (*cherkeska*) of dark-green cloth, reaching to 2 vershoks [3-1/2 inches] below the knees, without a standing collar or cuffs, of the same pattern as for Caucasian Cossack Host regiments, trimmed with red edging along the front opening to the bottoms of both skirts and along the lower end of the sleeves; closed with small hooks from the cartridge-holders to the waist. The *beshmet* to the coat is of red stamin and 1 vershok [1-3/4 inch] shorter than it. Black cartridge-holders on the coat (each for 8 cartridges), leather, surrounded with red worsted tape; tube of birch with brass caps. Shoulder straps of red cloth with the battery number cut out on yellow cloth; shoulder strap buttons of yellow brass with the raised image of two crossed cannons and the battery number, as prescribed for batteries of Army field artillery. *Sharovary* pants of dark-green cloth with leather foot straps and a red edge along the seam. pistol lanyard of red wool. Pistol holder—upper part of red cloth and lower part of dark green. Circassian *burka* instead of a greatcoat. The girdle is a black strap 1/2 vershoks [7/8 inch] wide, with a frog for the dagger and brass fittings.

Circassian sword belt of black leather with brass fittings. Circassian pistol of any pattern. Circassian *shashka* sword similar to the *shashka* for Caucasian Line Cossack regiments. Circassian dagger decorated as the owner pleases.

The saddle consists of a tree, girth, stirrup straps with stirrups, saddle cloth, crupper, surcingle, and valise with pillow. The valise and pillow on the saddle are of black leather and trimmed along the edges with red morocco. Bridle of rawhide leather with brass fittings. The halter is made from a rawhide strap. Circassian *nagaika* whip (Illus. 1214).

### Non-commissioned officers [uryadniki].

The same headdress as for cossacks but with the top trimmed with gold galloon. The same cossack pattern coat but the upper part to the waist trimmed with gold galloon, as well as the lower end of the sleeves. The *beshmet* to the coat has gold galloon trim around the collar and to the waist. Cartridge-holders on the coat, shoulder straps, *sharovary*, and all other items are exactly the same as for cossacks (Illus. 1215).

### Officers.

The *beshmet* to the coat is of the pattern for lower ranks but of red shalloon instead of red stamin. Cartridge-holders on the coat (each holding 8 cartridges) are black velvet with inside pockets trimmed round with wide gold lace; tubes of Karelian birch with gilt caps. Gold scaled epaulettes with the field the same, on which is the battery number, as is also on the buttons with their image of two crossed cannons. *Sharovary* pants the same as for lower ranks but trimmed down the side seams with two rows of gold galloon, between which, along the seam, is a red strip. Silver pistol lanyard. Pistol holder as for lower ranks but trimmed along the edges with gold galloon. Girdle of red lace tape interwoven with gold, 1/2 vershok [7/8 inch] wide, with a grease-box and loop for the dagger; silvered fittings. Sword belt of the pattern for lower ranks but with silvered fittings. *Shashka* sword with a silver sword knot. Valise and pillow pad on the saddle trimmed along the edges with gold galloon in addition to the red morocco. Bridle with brass fittings. Headdress, coat, pistol, and all other items of the patterns for lower ranks without any alterations (Illus. 1215) (18).

Apart from the changes in uniforms described here for all units of the Caucasian Line Cossack Host, all directives regarding the standard **general officer's uniform** and uniforms for **general-adjutants** and **aides-de-camp to H.I.M.**, **staff duty officers**, and **adjutants** in the Don Host—set forth above in the chapter for that host—also apply to the Caucasian Line Cossack Host.

## IV. THE ASTRAKHAN COSSACK HOST. [*ASTRAKHANSKOE KAZACHE VOISKO.*]

REGIMENTS

**1 January 1827** - In order to differentiate between **ranks**, small stamped stars are established for officers' epaulettes, as for regular forces (19).

**10 July 1827** - Regiments in the Astrakhan Cossack Host are ordered to have round **pompons** on the headdress: of white thread [*belye nityanye*] for lower ranks (later replaced by woollen), silver for officers. (By a misunderstanding these pompons were introduced only for non-commissioned officers [*uryadniki*] and officers, and privates began to wear them only from 1829) (20).

**15 November 1827** - **Shoulder straps** are established for lower ranks, with the cut-out number of the regiment backed by red cloth (21). Throughout the Host cords on **headdresses** are removed (21).

**27 August 1829** - For officers **epaulettes** with a scaled field are established, of the pattern for regular light cavalry, with a gilt numeral denoting the number of the regiment (22).

**15 November 1829** - Regiments in the **Astrakhan Cossack Host** are prescribed the same uniform clothing as given to them on 11 October 1817 (dark blue with lemon [*limonnyi*] trim), 1 January 1827, 10 July 1827, and 7 August 1829, except with white pompons changed to lemon colored, black girdles changed to lemon and white with a mix of black and orange, pistol lanyards changed to lemon with a mix of black color, except for non-commissioned officers who keep the present colors of this cord's tassels and slides: white with black and orange. Along with these changes the HIGHEST monogram on the cartridge pouch cover is removed. Saddlecloths and cushions, regarding which there had previously been no regulations, are ordered to be of the pattern for the Don Host, dark blue in color with lemon trim. (Illus. 1216 and 1217) (23).

**April 1831 - Officers without permanent positions** [*za-uryad-ofitsery*] are to have small stamped stars on their epaulettes to distinguish rank, like those introduced on 1 January 1827 (24).

**15 July 1837** - Officers are given a new pattern **sash** with a narrow silver lace [*tes'ma*] body with three stripes of light-orange and black silk, as for regular forces (25).

**17 December 1837** - Following the example of regular forces, officers' **epaulettes** are given an additional fourth thin twist of braid (26).

**29 April 1838** - The following are prescribed for the **Astrakhan Host**:

**Lower ranks.**
Headdresses of the previous pattern. ammunition pouches instead of cartridge pouches [*patrontashi vmesto lyadunok*], for 40 rounds, of black Russian leather, with a lid of the same, and a cross strap of black rawhide.
Pistols of the pattern for light cavalry; pistol holders or carriers (instead of holsters) [*chushki ili kobury vmesto ol'stredei*] of polished black leather; pistol lanyards the same color as the edging on the uniform; the upper part of the pistol case to the lock is of cloth the same color as the collar, while the lower part is of polished black leather. Sword belts of the same leather. *Shashkas* (instead of sabers) with hilt, rings, bands, and brass endpieces, in a wooden scabbard wrapped with black leather. In mounted order a musket of the pattern for the L.-Gds. Black Sea Squadron, with a case, worn behind the back over the right shoulder on a black rawhide cross strap 5/8 vershok [1-1/10 inches] wide, with a brass buckle.
Saddlecloths and cushions on the saddle the same color as the uniform, with a canvas lining, trimmed (around the edges of the saddlecloth and along the seams around the cushion) with lemon colored tape 7/8 vershok [1-1/2 inches] wide, with a length of the same tape 9-1/2 vershoks [16-5/8 inches] long on the rear corners of the saddlecloth. Valise of gray cloth, 14-1/2 vershoks [24-1/2 inches] long and 12-3/4 vershoks [22-1/3 inches] in circumference, with a canvas lining and four white metal buttons; on the buttons a raised image of the regimental number (Illus. 1218).

**Officers.**
Headdress of the previous pattern. ammunition pouch (instead of cartridge pouch) for 20 rounds, of black morocco, with a lid of the same and a crossbelt of silver lace without any light or stripe, lined with black morocco.
Pistols of the pattern for light cavalry officers. Pistol holders of black morocco; silver pistol lanyards; the upper part of the pistol case to the lock of cloth the same color as the collar, the lower of black morocco. Sword belt of silver lace without any light, lined with black morocco. Shashka (instead of saber) with gilt hilt, bands, rings, and endpiece, in a wooden scabbard wrapped with black morocco (Illus. 1219).
Saddlecloths and cushion on the saddle the same color as the uniform, lined with black calf-skin and trimmed (along the edges of the saddlecloth and along the seams around the cushion) with lace the same color as the edges of the coat, 3/4 vershoks [1-1/4 inches] wide, 5-1/2 vershoks [9-5/8 inches] long on the front corners and 9 [15-3/4] on the rear corners. Gray cloth valise 12 vershoks [21 inches] long and 9 [15-3/4] in circumference, with leather lining and four silver buttons; on the buttons a raised image of the regimental number.
For lower ranks as well as officers, pistols are ordered to be carried in a holder fastened to the sword belt behind the back, near the left side, but they were to be worn—as well as the holder, cord, and case—only when in full uniform [*pri polnoi forme*].
Horse harness for lower ranks is prescribed to be arranged so that the valise and horse cloth [*popona*] are behind the saddle; the horse cloth is to be stowed under the valise and together with it lashed to the saddle with three black straps with brass double-sided buckles of the previous pattern; the greatcoat is in front of the saddle and tied to it with three of the same straps with buckles; the rolling of the greatcoat and the stowing of other items, as well as all uniform clothing, accouterments, and weapons not mentioned here, including the cover for the headdress, are left unchanged (27).

**2 January 1844** - A metal **cockade** is established for the front of the band on officers' forage caps, as for officers' caps in regular forces (28).

**20 May 1844** - With the general allocation of colors for **forage caps** throughout the Military establishment, dark-blue forage caps are established for the Astrakhan Cossack Host, with a yellow band and yellow piping around the top (29).

**6 January 1845** - By the Administrative Regulation for the **Astrakhan Cossack Host** laid down on this date, its regiments are prescribed the following uniforms, weapons, and horse furniture.

**Lower ranks.**

Headdress of black lamb's fleece with a yellow cloth crown and a chinstrap; yellow woolen pompon, with yellow cloth lining on a lower pompon [*repeika*]; black neckcloth; very dark-blue cloth chekmen with yellow piping around the collar and cuffs; very dark-blue sharovary pants with yellow stripes; yellow shalloon [*shalonovyi*] girdle; gray cloth greatcoat with yellow tabs on the collar; boots with iron spurs; yellow shoulder straps with a red regimental number and white metal buttons; red leather sword knot; forage cap of very dark-blue cloth with yellow band and piping, no visor.

ammunition pouch for 40 rounds in tin holders laid in two rows, lined with black leather, with a lid of the same leather and stitching along the edges. Crossbelt for the ammunition pouch of black rawhide leather, 3/4 vershoks [1-1/4 inches] wide, with a brass buckle, slide, and endpiece.

Carrier for stowing the pistol - of black leather with two side flaps, with stitching along the edges, 4 vershoks [7 inches] long on the left side and 5 [8-3/4] on the right, 4 vershoks [7 inches] wide at the top and 1-3/4 [3] at the bottom; pistol lanyard of yellow wool with one tassel and two slides, 2 arshins 7 veshoks [68-1/4 inches] long. Pistol case of dark-blue cloth to the lower part of the lock, and from the bottom of shiny black leather upwards to the middle where the cloth ends; the case is trimmed around with dark-blue tape; for tying around the butt - a yellow woolen cord with tassel; length of the cases 9-1/2 vershoks [16-5/8 inches], width at the top 3-1/2 [6-1/8] and at the bottom 1-3/4 [3]; below, the circumference of the bottom is 2-1/2 vershoks [4-3/8 inches]; tape on the cases is 1/4 vershok [1/2 inch] wide. Sword belt of shiny black leather with three brass buckles; width of the strap - 6/8 vershok [1-1/4 inches].

Saddlecloth of dark-blue army cloth with canvas lining, trimmed around the edges with yellow cloth tape 7/8 vershok [1-1/2 inches] wide. The same tape is laid on the rear corners of the saddlecloth, 9-1/2 vershoks [16-5/8 inches] in length. Cushion of dark-blue army cloth with canvas lining, trimmed along the seams with yellow cloth tape 7/8 vershok [1-1/2 inches] wide.

Valise of gray army cloth with canvas lining, four white metal buttons with the regimental number. Length of the valise - 14-1/2 vershoks [24-1/2 inches], the ends 12-3/4 vershoks [22-1/3 inches] in circumference.

Saddle and harness of the usual cossack pattern; bridle, harness, and chest-band [*uzda, pafy i nagrudnik*] without any fittings; saddle-blanket [*potnik*] with cover of thick white linen, in five layers, covered above, trimmed with black calf-leather along the edges below; surcingle [*v'yuchnyi remen'*] of black rawhide with a brass buckle, 1 arshin 7 vershoks [40-1/4 inches] long.

Shashka sword - handle, bands with rings, and endpiece—of brass; wooden scabbard, wrapped in black leather, without a case; pistol of the pattern adopted in the cavalry, with a case sewn into the pistol carrier, worn on the waist on the left; musket with its sling, confirmed on 29 April 1838; musket case of black shaggy felt [*burka*] with a strap of black rawhide leather 3/8 vershok [5/8 inch] wide; horse-cloth [*popon*] of gray cloth; lance [*drotik*] with a dark-green shaft.

For clerks and non-commissioned officers there is silver galloon on the collar and cuffs. For trumpeters the coat and for non-commissioned officers the tassels on cords and cases are according to the confirmed patterns.

**Officers.**

Silver pompon on the headdress, lower pompon lined with yellow cloth; very dark-blue cloth chekmen, with silver buttonhole loops and yellow piping on the collar and cuffs; yellow silk girdle, silver epaulettes, according to the confirmed pattern; silver sash of the confirmed pattern; silver sword knot on silk lace; forage cap the same as for lower ranks but with a visor.

Ammunition pouch for 20 rounds in tin holders laid out in one row and lined with black morocco leather; ammunition pouch trimmed from the bottom along the seam with thin black silk cord, with a black morocco lid trimmed along the edge with silver lace without a light; ammunition pouch belt of silver lace without a light, lined with black morocco, 11/16 vershok [1-1/5 inches] wide, with silver buckles, slides, and endpieces.

Carrier for stowing the pistol, of black morocco with two flaps, with stitching along the edges, 1-7/8 vershoks [3-1/4 inches] long on the left side, 3-1/2 [6-1/8] on the right; 3 vershoks [5-1/4 inches] wide at the top, 1-1/2 [2-5/8] at the bottom; silver pistol lanyard with one tassel and two slides, length 2 arshins 10 vershoks [73-1/2 inches]. Pistol case of dark-blue cloth to the lower part of the lock, the rest of black morocco; upwards, to the middle where the cloth ends, and below at the very bottom—trimmed around with silver lace without a light; for tying around the butt—a black silk cord; length of the case 7 vershoks [12-1/4 inches], 3-3/4 [6-1/2] wide at the top, 1-3/4 [3] wide in the middle, and 2 vershoks [3-1/2 inches] in circumference at the bottom; the lace on the cases is 3-3/8 vershoks [5-9/10 inches] wide. Sword belt of the pattern confirmed for light cavalry, modified so that the waist strap is whole and the slings sewn to it by means of an oval ring which is only half visible; the sword belt itself is sewn to the waist belt with silver lace without a light.

Dark-blue cloth saddlecloth lined with black calf-leather, trimmed along the edges with yellow tape 3/4 vershok [1-1/4 inches] wide; the same tape in the corners of the saddlecloth: 5-1/2 vershoks [9-5/8 inches] long in the front corners and 9 [15-3/4] in the rear; dark-blue cloth pillow lined around with black calf-leather and trimmed along the seam with yellow tape 3/4 vershok [1-1/4 inches] wide. Gray cloth valise with leather reinforcement, with four white metal buttons with the regimental number; the valise is 12 vershoks [21 inches] long, its ends 9 vershoks [15-3/4 inches] around.

Shashka - handle, bands with rings, and all other items according to the patterns for lower ranks, except for the musket with its sling, case, and lance, which are not prescribed for officers (Illus. 1220 and 1221) (30).

**14 April 1845** - Chekmens in the Astrakhan Host are replaced with **jackets**, as in the Don Host. Along with this officers are ordered to wear their **pistols** with cords only when in formation (31).

**27 April 1845** - As a consequence of the change on 14 April 1845 in the uniforms of the **Astrakhan Host**, it is laid down that: the chekmen is to be dark blue in color, as before, but in length reaching to 4 vershoks [7 inches] above the knee, with a yellow edge on the collar and cuffs, and for officers the addition of their prescribed silver buttonhole loops; headdress of black fleece 4-1/2 vershoks [7-7/8 inches] high without an indentation on top, with a yellow cloth bag under which is sewn an oilcloth base; yellow girdle; pistol lanyard of the previous pattern but sewn to the carrier that is attached to the sword belt on the left side (Illus. 1220 and 1221). The rest of the items of uniform clothing and weaponry, as well as horse furniture, remain unchanged (32).

## ARTILLERY.

**1 January 1827** - In order to differentiate between **ranks**, small stamped stars are established for officers' epaulettes, as for regular forces (33).

**7 August 1829** - **Epaulettes** with scaled fields are established for officers' uniforms, of the pattern for epaulettes in the regular light cavalry (34).

**15 November 1829** - According to new confirmation of the uniform patterns for **Astrakhan Cossack artillery**, it is prescribed the same uniform clothing and weaponry as horse artillery companies of the Don artillery, but with the following distinctions: headdress without cords; shoulder straps and epaulettes with the number 7; instead of red stripes on the sharovary pants—lemon colored; on the rear corners of saddlecloths are added the HIGHEST monogram in yellow cloth, trimmed with red cord (Illus. 1222) (35).

**15 July 1837** - Officers are given new pattern **sashes** with narrow silver lace with three stripes of light-orange and black silk, as for regular forces (36).

**17 December 1837** - To officers' **epaulettes** is added, following the example of the regular forces, a fourth thin twist of braid (37).

**29 April 1838** - The **changes** promulgated on this date and described above in regard to the uniforms and weapons of Don Horse-Artillery batteries are extended with equal force to the artillery of the Astrakhan Cossack Host, except for the stripes on the sharovary pants, which in the Astrakhan artillery remain lemon colored, as before (Illus. 1223) (38).

**22 May 1838** - With the change in **numbering** in Cossack Horse Artillery, the Astrakhan Cossack Host's artillery half-battery is prescribed No. 13 on epaulettes and shoulder straps instead of No. 7 (39).

**2 January 1844** - A metal **cockade** is established for the front of the band on officers' forage caps, as for officers' caps in regular forces (40).

**6 January 1845** - According to the administrative regulation of this date for the **Astrakhan Cossack Host**, the Horse-Artillery battery (No. 16) is prescribed uniforms, weapons, and horse furniture completely identical to that confirmed on 20 April 1838 and 14 and 27 April 1845 for horse-artillery batteries of the Don Host, as set forth in detail above (see Don Host artillery) (41).

**27 April 1845** - Following the example of the Don Host, for the **Astrakhan Cossack artillery** (its Horse-Artillery Battery No. 16) are established: chekmen of dark-green cloth with collar and cuffs of black cloth, reaching to 4 vershoks [7 inches] above the knee; on the collar, cuffs, and down the front an edging of red cloth; headdress of black fleece 4-1/2 vershoks [7-7/8 inches] high without an indentation, with a scarlet cloth bag under which is sewn an oilcloth base. Pistol case of the previous pattern, but sewn to the carrier which is fastened to the sword belt on the left side. The remaining items of uniform clothing and weaponry, as well as horse furniture, remain unchanged (42).

**8 July 1852** - **Chekmens** in Horse-Artillery batteries are ordered to be made following the example of the Don and Caucasian Cossack artillery with a red edge down the front opening (43).

Apart from the changes in uniform described here for all units of the Astrakhan Cossack Host, all orders promulgated in regard to the **standard general-officer's uniform** and the uniforms for **general-adjutants**, **aides-de-camp of H.I.M.**, and **adjutants** to Don Host generals, set forth above in the section for that Host, also apply to the Astrakhan Cossack Host.

## V. THE URAL COSSACK HOST. [*URAL'SKOE KAZACHE VOISKO.*]

REGIMENTS

**1 January 1827** - In order to differentiate between **ranks**, small stamped stars are established for officers' epaulettes, as for regular forces (44).

**7 August 1829** - **Epaulettes** with scaled fields are established for officers' uniforms, of the pattern for epaulettes in the regular light cavalry (45).

**15 November 1829** - Regiments in the **Ural Host** are prescribed the same uniforms as confirmed on this date for the Astrakhan Host and described above in the section for that Host, with the lemon color changed everywhere to **light blue** [*svetlosinii*] and the red numbers on the shoulder straps changed to white (Illus. 1224 and 1225) (46).

**April 1831** - **Officers without permanent positions** [*za-uryad-ofitsery*] are to have small stamped stars on their epaulettes to distinguish rank, like those introduced on 1 January 1827 (47).

**15 July 1837** - Officers are given a new pattern **sash** of narrow silver lace [*tesma*] with three stripes of light-orange and black silk, as for regular forces (48).

**17 December 1837** - Following the example of regular forces, officers' **epaulettes** are given an additional fourth thin twist of braid (49).

**29 April 1838** - The **changes** in uniforms and weapons promulgated on this date for the regiments of the Astrakhan Host are extended with equal force to the regiments of the Ural Host, except for its prescribed distinctive colors (Illus. 1226) (50).

**2 January 1844** - A metal **cockade** is established for the front of the band on officers' forage caps, as for officers' caps in regular forces (51).

**20 May 1844** - With the general allocation of colors for **forage caps** throughout the Military establishment, dark-blue forage caps are established for the Ural Host, with a light-blue band and light-blue piping around the top (52).

**14 April 1845** - Chekmens in the Ural Host are replaced with **jackets** of the pattern established for Cossack generals when in Host uniform. Along with this, Ural Cossack regiments, when on service in the Caucasus, are permitted to wear headdresses of the pattern for the Caucasian Line Cossack Host. Officers are ordered to wear pistols with cords only when in formation (53).

**27 April 1845** - As a consequence of the change on 14 April 1845 in the uniforms of the **Ural Host**, the following uniform is established: dark-blue chekmen, as before, but in length reaching to 4 vershoks [7 inches] above the knee, with a light-blue edge on the collar and cuffs, and for officers the addition of their prescribed silver buttonhole loops; headdress of black fleece 4-1/2 vershoks [7-7/8 inches] high without an indentation on top, with a light-blue cloth bag under which is sewn an oilcloth base; light-blue girdle; pistol lanyard of the previous pattern but sewn to the carrier that is attached to the sword belt on the left side. The rest of the items of uniform clothing and weaponry, as well as horse furniture, remain unchanged (Illus. 1227) (54).

## LIFE-GUARDS URAL SOTNIA.

(Until 6 April 1830 this was the Leib-Ural Sotnia, being renamed the Life-Guards Ural Sotnia on this date. On 25 September 1846 it was named the Life-Guards Ural Squadron, and on 17 August 1847—the Life-Guards Ural Cossack Double-Squadron)

**15 April 1826** - White thread **plumes** were established for the Leib-Ural Sotnia in place of white hair plumes. Officers were given silver **pompons**. Instead of black **accouterments**—white, according to the patterns for the L.-Gds. Cossack Regiment (Illus. 1228 and 1229) (55).

**1 January 1827** - In order to differentiate between **ranks**, small stamped stars are established for officers' epaulettes, as for regular forces (56).

**13 December 1828** - **Epaulettes** with a scaled field and a hanging white fringe are established for lower ranks (Illus. 1230) (57).

**7 August 1829** - **Epaulettes** with scaled fields are established for officers' uniforms, of the pattern for epaulettes in the regular light cavalry (58).

**4 July 1837** - On all those occasions when in the regular forces frock coats are allowed to be worn, officers of the L.-Gds. Ural Sotnia, apart from the coat with buttonhole loops, are permitted to wear a **chekmen** without embroidery: dark blue without any piping, as established on 28 October 1836 for the L.-Gds. Cossack Regiment (59).

**15 July 1837** - Officers are given new pattern **sashes** with narrow silver lace with three stripes of light-orange and black silk, as for regular forces (60).

**17 December 1837** - To officers' **epaulettes** is added, following the example of the regular forces, a fourth thin twist of braid (61).

**29 April 1838** - For the **L.-Gds. Ural Sotnia** there are established:

**Lower ranks.**

Headdresses without cords, with a plate of white tin of the pattern prescribed on this date for the L.-Gds. Cossack Regiment; iron epaulettes without a fringe, with a backing of light-blue cloth.

Ammunition pouch (instead of cartridge pouch) for 40 rounds, of black Russian leather, with a lid of the same and a deerskin crossbelt, without any ornamentation; pistols of the pattern adopted in the light cavalry; pistol carriers or holders (instead of holsters) of shiny black leather; pistol lanyards of light-blue wool; the upper part of the pistol cases to the firelock to be of light-blue cloth; the lower part of shiny black leather; sword belts of red Russian leather; shashkas (instead of sabers) with brass handle, bands, rings, and endpieces in wooden scabbards wrapped with black leather; muskets (instead of carbines) for mounted order, after the pattern for the L.-Gds. Black Sear Squadron, with cases; muskets to be worn behind the back on a rawhide belt over the right shoulder, 5/8 vershok [1-1/10 inches] wide, with a brass buckle (Illus. 1231).

**Officers.**

Headdresses without cords and with the same decoration as for lower ranks but in silver.

Ammunition pouches (instead of cartridge pouches) of black morocco with a lid of light-blue cloth, with a crossbelt of silver lace without any light, backed by black morocco; pistols of the pattern adopted by officers in the light cavalry; pistol carriers of black morocco; silver pistol lanyards; the upper part of the pistol cases of light-blue cloth, the lower part of black morocco; sword belt of silver lace without any light, lined with black morocco; shashk (instead of saber) with gilt handle, bands, rings, and endpieces, in a wooden scabbard wrapped with black morocco (Illus. 1232).

Following the example of the L.-Gds. Cossack Regiment, officers as well as lower ranks in the sotnia are ordered to carry the pistol in its carrier, fastened to the sword belt in back near the left side, but they are to carry it, as well as the carrier, cord, and case, only when in full uniform. Lower ranks' horse furniture is prescribed to be fitted according to the directions established at this time for the L.-Gds. Cossack Regiment. All items of uniform clothing, accouterments, and weaponry not mentioned here, including the cover for the headdress, remain unchanged, except for collars and cuffs on winter and summer coats, to which is added piping of light-blue cloth following the pattern for the winter coat of H.I.M. the Heir and Tsesarevich's Ataman Regiment, and also except for greatcoats, which the sotnia is ordered to have the same as for that regiment (62).

**2 January 1844** - A metal **cockade** is established for the band on officers' forage caps, as for officers' caps in regular forces (63).

**20 May 1844** - With the general allocation of **forage cap** colors throughout the Military Administration, dark-blue caps are established for the L.-Gds. Ural Sotnia, with a light-blue band and light-blue piping around the top (64).

**14 April 1845** - Jackets are withdrawn from the L.-Gds. Ural Sotnia. Only chekmens are left for both ceremonial and everyday occasions. Officers are ordered to wear pistols with cords only when in formation (65).

**27 April 1845** - Consequent to the **changes** in uniform of 14 April 1845 for the L.-Gds. Ural Sotnia, there are established:

**Lower ranks.**

Coat [*mundir*] of the pattern of the previous winter coats except reaching to 2 vershoks [3-1/2 inches] above the knee; headdress of black astrakhan 4-1/2 vershoks [7-7/8 inches] high, without an indentation, with a bag of light-blue cloth, under which is sewn an oilcloth base; ammunition pouch of the pattern for H.I.M. the Heir and Tsesarevich's Ataman Regiment, i.e. of black lacquered leather, on a white elkskin belt, for 20 rounds in two rows; pistol of the pattern for H.I.M. the Heir and Tsesarevich's Ataman Regiment, i.e. on a light-blue cord and in a case of light-blue cloth sewn to a leather holder worn on the sword belt on the left side, and not behind the back (Illus. 1233).

**Officers.**

Coat and shashka sword of the patterns for lower ranks; ammunition pouch and pistol of the previous pattern, but with the pistol case sewn to the holder; worn on the left side on the sword belt; the undress chekmen [*vitsechekmen'*] for officers, the sharovary pants for officers and lower ranks, and all other items of uniform and weaponry not mentioned here, as well as horse harness, remain unchanged (66).

**27 February 1847** - The L.-Gds. Ural Squadron is ordered to have **shabracks** as for other Guards Cossack troops (67).

**18 January 1848** - A pattern for officers' **cartridge pouches** [*lyadunki*] is confirmed in place of the carriers [*patrontashi*] (68).

**27 January 1848** - For the L.-Gds. Ural Double-Squadron a sky-blue **parade coat** [*goluboi paradnyi mundir*] with a dark-blue collar is established (Ilus. 1234) (69).

**15 January 1851** - It is ordered that: the **musket sling** be made of two rawhide straps with one side blackened, joined together by a brass buckle and fastened to the musket by the ends being passed through the stock; the musket case be of black Russian leather lined with gray cloth and have a rawhide strap opposite the hammer; the brass kettle be carried on the right side of the valise instead of the left, in order to avoid damaging the musket and shashka; officers are not to have holsters, and **pistols** are to be in a carrier of the present pattern; lower ranks, when going out on guard duty, are to have the musket worn over the shoulder (70).

**1 May 1852** - The establishment of the L.-Gds. Ural Cossack Double-Squadron is ordered to have, following the example of the L.-Gds. Black Sea Cossack Double-Squadron, 6 **trumpeters**, who are always to be on duty with the squadron of the L.-Gds. Ural Double-Squadron that is in St. Petersburg (71).

Apart from the changes in uniform described here for all units of the Ural Cossack Host, all orders promulgated in regard to the **standard general-officer's uniform** and the uniforms for **general-adjutants**, **aides-de-camp of H.I.M.**, and **adjutants** to Don Host generals, set forth above, also apply to the Ural Cossack Host.

## VI. THE ORENBURG COSSACK HOST. [*ORENBURGSKOE KAZACHE VOISKO.*]

### REGIMENTS

**1 January 1827** - In order to differentiate between **ranks**, small stamped stars are established for officers' epaulettes, as for regular forces (72).

**7 August 1829** - **Epaulettes** with scaled fields are established for officers' uniforms, of the pattern for epaulettes in the regular light cavalry (73).

**15 November 1829** - Regiments in the Orenburg Cossack Host are prescribed the same uniforms as confirmed on this date for the Ural Host and described above in the section for that Host, except with the light-blue color changed everywhere to **raspberry** (Illus. 1235) (74).

**April 1831** - **Officers without permanent positions** [*zauryad-ofitsery*] are to have small stamped stars on their epaulettes to distinguish rank, like those introduced on 1 January 1827 (75).

**4 November 1833** - In regiments of the Orenburg Cossack Host **saddle-trees** [*lenchiki*] are removed from saddles. In place of the previous carbines, they are given **muskets** of the new pattern established for the Black Sea Host, likewise carried over the back on a black sling (76).

**21 March 1835** - With the establishment, instead of two Teptyar Cossack regiments, of one cossack regiment included in the Orenburg Cossack Host under the title of the **First Orenburg** and made up of 8 active squadrons, 1 reserve squadron, and 1 noncombatant company, its personnel are prescribed the following uniforms, accouterments, and weaponry:

**Lower combatant ranks.**
Headdress of the pattern for the Don Host but with a falling bag, upper and lower pompons of light-blue cloth; gray cloth greatcoat with a light-blue collar; dark-green cloth jacket with light-blue piping on the collar and cuffs, and shoulder straps of the same color; sharovary pants of dark-green cloth with light-blue stripes; light-blue girdle; carbine, pistol, lance with pennant—the top white and bottom light blue; saber (Illus. 1236).

**Officers.**
Officers have the same uniform as lower ranks but with a single silver buttonhole loop on each side of the jacket's collar, with two buttonholes on the cuffs and the other distinctions for officers (Illus. 1237).

**Noncombatant ranks.**
Gray forage cap with a similar band, with two light-blue lines of piping and a visor; gray cloth greatcoat and half-caftan with dark-green collar and light-blue shoulder straps; gray riding trousers with light-blue piping (Illus. 1238) (77).

**15 July 1837** - Officers are given a new pattern **sash** of narrow silver lace with three stripes of light-orange and black silk, as for regular forces (78).

**17 December 1837** - Officers' **epaulettes** are given an additional fourth thin twist of braid (79).

**29 April 1838** - The **changes** in uniforms and weapons promulgated on this date for the regiments of the Astrakhan Cossack Host and described above are extended with equal force to the regiments of the Orenburg Cossack Host, except for its prescribed distinctive colors (Illus. 1239 and 1240), and the 1st Orenburg Regiment's lance pennants are kept (80).

**12 December 1840** - With the confirmation on this date of an Administrative Regulation for the **Orenburg Cossack Host**, all regiments of the Host (No. 1 through 10) are prescribed uniform clothing, weapons, and horse furniture in accordance with the pattern confirmed on 21 March 1835 for the 1st Orenburg Cossack Regiment, in which at this same time pennants are removed from lances. Shoulder straps are to have the number assigned to that regiment (81).

**13 April 1842** - With the renaming of the 1st Orenburg Cossack Regiment as the **Ufa Cossack Regiment**, it is ordered that the shoulder straps of that unit's lower ranks have, instead of a number, the Cyrillic letters U K. Buttons are smooth, as for other regiments (82).

**12 October 1843** - The following are established for lower ranks of the Orenburg Cossack Host who are transferred to **internal service** within the Host:

**Mounted lower ranks.**
Dark-green cloth forage cap with a light-blue band and light-blue piping; gray cloth greatcoat with a light-blue collar; gray cloth sharovary pants with light-blue piping; ammunition pouch, sword belt, and shashka sword of the patterns for serving cossacks; pistol with cord of the normal pattern; saddle as for serving cossacks, without the cloth shabrack (Illus. 1241).

**Lower ranks on foot.**
Forage cap, greatcoat, and sharovary as for mounted cossacks; a lance 2-1/2 arshins [70 inches] long (Illus. 1241) (83).

**20 October 1843** - Following the example of lower ranks in regular light cavalry regiments, lower ranks of the Ufa Cossack Regiment are ordered to have **muskets** when in dismounted formation, as well as when on guard duties (84).

**2 January 1844** - A metal **cockade** is ordered to be worn on the band on officers' forage caps in the Orenburg Cossack Host, as established at this same time for officer' caps in regular forces (85).

**7 January 1844** - On this date the following uniform and weaponry in the **Ufa Cossack Regiment** is confirmed for a non-combatant company officer and for government authorized orderlies [*kazennye denshchiki*]:

**Officers of the Ufa Cossack Regiment's noncombatant company.**
Gray cloth chekmen with light-blue collar and cuffs; gray cloth sharovary pants with light-blue stripes; headdress, upper and lower pompons, epaulettes, pistol, pistol lanyard, girdle, and shashka sword—the same as for combatant officers of the Ufa Cossack Regiment (Illus. 1243).

**Authorized orderlies in the Ufa Cossack Regiment.**
Dark-green cloth chekmen, with lining of the same color as the chekmen; standing collar fastened by small hooks, as is the front opening; sharovary pants and boots the same as worn by the officers to whom the orderly is attached; gray cloth greatcoat of soldier pattern but without shoulder straps and with an officer's cape, with sewn-on stripes of the color of the coat collar of the officer to whom the orderly is attached; forage cap of the pattern for soldiers, with light-blue on the seams along the sides and on the crown (86).

**20 May 1844** - With the general allocation of colors for **forage caps** throughout the Military establishment, dark-green caps are established for the Orenburg and Ufa Cossack Regiments (the latter would be disbanded on 29 September 1845), with a light-blue band and light-blue piping around the top (87).

**14 April 1845** - Chekmens are replaced with **jackets** of the pattern established for Cossack generals when in Host uniform. Officers are ordered to wear pistols with cords only when in formation (88).

**27 April 1845** - As a consequence of the change on 14 April 1845 in the uniforms of the **Orenburg Cossack Host**, the following uniform is established: dark-green chekmen, as before, but in length reaching to 4 vershoks [7 inches] above the knee, with a light-blue edge on the collar and cuffs, and for officers the addition of their prescribed silver buttonhole loops; headdress of black fleece 4-1/2 vershoks [7-7/8 inches] high without an indentation on top, with a light-blue cloth bag under which is sewn an oilcloth base; light-blue girdle; pistol lanyard of the previous pattern but sewn to the carrier that is attached to the sword belt on the left side (Illus. 1244). The rest of the items of uniform clothing and weaponry, as well as horse furniture, remain unchanged (89).

**6 October 1854** - Uniforms and arms are confirmed for the newly formed **foot battalions** of the Orenburg Cossack Host (Illus. 1245).

**Officers.**

Headdress of sky-blue cloth, the top rounded and quilted, trimmed around with silver lace 1/2 vershok [7/8 inch] wide, brim of black sheep's fleece, chinstrap of black leather 1/2 vershok wide. Dark-green cloth forage cap with two lines of sky-blue piping around the top and above the band, with a visor. Black silk neckcloth with a bib [*manishka*]. Dark-green coat with light-blue piping around the collar and cuffs, closed with small hooks; behind and on the sides with four pleats [*skladki*] with pockets between them; skirts to reach to 5 vershoks [8-3/4 inches] above the knee; two silver buttonhole loops on the cuffs and one on the collar. Chekmen of the same cloth and cut as the coat, but without buttonhole loops. Standard army cossack ammunition pouch, for 20 rounds; lid and cartridges of black morocco; lid trimmed with silver galloon; crossbelt of silver galloon backed with black morocco, with silver mountings. The ammunition pouch is worn over the left shoulder so that its right end comes under the arm in the middle third of the right side of the body, and the left end—in the direction of the left shoulder.

Silver epaulettes; battalion number on a sky-blue field; backed with cloth, likewise sky blue, and fastened with a smooth white metal button. Belt of silver lace 6/8 vershok [1-1/4 inches] wide with silver fittings and backed with black morocco. Dark-green sharovary pants with sky-blue piping and two pockets. Summer sharovary of thin white linen, of the same cut as the winter sharovary. Greatcoat of the normal officer pattern with a gray cloth hood and collar, with sky-blue edging along the collar and smooth white metal buttons. Army boots.

Shashka sword - according to the description confirmed on 29 April 1838. Infantry sword knot. Silver sword belt, without any light, backed with black morocco, with silver fittings; worn over the shoulder. Cavalry pistol. Carrier for stowing the pistol - of black morocco; to be worn at the waist on the left side even with the shashka. Pistol case - the top part of dark-green cloth; trimmed with narrow silver lace where it fastens; the lower part of black morocco; trimmed with the same lace where the cloth joins the leather and at the end of the leather; tied with a black silk cord with a tassel. pistol lanyard - silver with a tassel. suede gloves.

**Cossacks.**

Headdress as for officers, of sky-blue army cloth; for non-commissioned officers [*uryadniki*] trimmed around with white thread lace and crossed on top with the same narrow lace; for cossacks trimmed only crosswise with narrow lace; brim and chinstrap as for officers. Dark-green forage cap of army cloth with two lines of sky-blue piping as for officers, but without a visor; on the band is cut out the company number. Black neckcloth of army cloth.

Chekmen (officer pattern) - of dark-green army cloth; the collar and interior of the chekmen to the waist is lined with linen; for non-commissioned officers the collar and cuffs are trimmed with silver army galloon; shoulder straps of sky-blue cloth with the battalion number cut out on yellow cloth.

Ammunition pouch of black Russian leather with holders for 40 rounds, of the pattern for Caucasus sappers; worn over the left shoulder on a crossbelt of white Russian leather under black polish, 6/8 vershok [1-1/4 inches] wide.

Belt of shiny black leather 6/8 vershok wide, with iron double and small buckles, endpiece, and slide, of the pattern for Black Sea Cossacks. Sharovary pants of dark-green army cloth with sky-blue piping and two pockets in the linen lining. Summer sharovary of army Flemish linen with two pockets made from lining linen, of the same pattern as winter sharovary. Soldier's greatcoat of standard pattern, of gray cloth, likewise the collar, which has sky-blue edging along the top; sky-blue shoulder straps of army cloth with the battalion number cut through on yellow cloth; smooth tin buttons. Army boots.

Standard infantry musket with bayonet. The bayonet scabbard is hung onto the belt by means of a frog in the manner for Black Sea Cossacks. The musket is also prescribed for non-commissioned officers. The musket sling and flint case [*ognivyi chekhol*] are of Russian leather polished black, following the patterns for regular troops. The gun-lock cover is the infantry pattern (in the case of percussion muskets being introduced it will be necessary to have firing nipple covers in accordance with the Minister of War's order of 13 December 1851).

Infantry knapsack, of calf-skin leather with straps of Russian leather polished black, 1 vershok [1-3/4 inches] wide; the straps are worn crossed over the chest in the manner of Tobolsk Cossacks. Iron pot and greatcoat strap. The iron pot is straped to the knapsack; over the knapsack is the greatcoat, rolled up in the infantry manner as for Tobolsk Cossacks; the straps for securing the pot and greatcoat are made of the same leather as the knapsack straps, the pot straps 1/2 vershok [7/8 inch] wide, the greatcoat straps 3/4 vershok [1-1/4]. (In the case of the battalions being armed with percussion muskets, it will be necessary to make a cut-out pocket under the knapsack cover flap for an iron case holding spare caps, as in the regular infantry.) Gloves - of dark-green cloth, of the pattern for army troops.

**Drummers.**

Headdress, forage cap, and neckcloth as for cossacks. Chekmen as for cossacks, but the breast, sleeves, and shoulder wings of sky-blue cloth; for musicians of non-commissioned officer rank the seams on the back are further trimmed with white army tape, according to the normal pattern for army drummers. Ammunition pouch of black Russian leather for 12 rounds, worn on a belt on the right side. Belt, winter and summer sharovary, greatcoat, boots, knapsack, iron pot, greatcoat strap, and gloves - as for cossacks. Drummer's crossbelt of white Russian leather under black polish, of the pattern for jäger regiments, 2-1/2 vershoks [4-3/8 inches] wide.

Cavalry pistol. Carriers of shiny black leather of the pattern for Black Sea Cossack battalions, worn on a belt between the knapsack and left thigh, with the butt turned under the left arm. Pistol case - the top of dark-green army cloth lined with linen, trimmed with narrow worsted sky-blue tape where it is fastened; lower part of shiny black leather with cloth trimmed with the same tape; closed with a sky-blue worsted cord with tassel. Worsted pistol lanyard, sky blue with a tassel (90).

## ARTILLERY

**1 January 1827** - In order to differentiate between **ranks**, small stamped stars are established for officers' epaulettes, as for regular forces (91).

**7 August 1829** - **Epaulettes** with scaled fields are established for officers' uniforms, of the pattern for epaulettes in the regular light cavalry (92).

**15 November 1829** - In the **Orenburg Cossack artillery** uniforms, arms, and horse furniture are established as in Don Horse-Artillery companies, except for headdress cords, which are not prescribed for the Orenburg artillery (Illus. 1246), and the replacement of yellow trim on lower ranks' saddlecloths by red (93).

**15 July 1837** - Officers are given new pattern **sashes** with narrow silver lace with three stripes of light-orange and black silk, as for regular forces (94).

**17 December 1837** - To officers' **epaulettes** is added, following the example of the regular forces, a fourth thin twist of braid (95).

**29 April 1838** - The **changes** in uniforms and arms for Don Horse-Artillery batteries, described above, are applied in equal measure to the artillery of the Orenburg Cossack Host (96).

**1 July 1839** - For lower ranks in **training detachments** of Orenburg Cossack Host horse-artillery batteries, the cadre of these detachments as well as the personnel rotated annually, there is established yellow tape around the epaulette, following the pattern confirmed for Instructional troops (97).

**26 January 1841** - By an Administrative Regulation confirmed on this date for the **Orenburg Cossack Host** its horse-artillery batteries (16, 17, and 18) are prescribed the same uniforms, weapons, and horse furniture as the previous Host batteries had (14 and 15), without any change except for the numbers on shoulder straps and officer' epaulettes (98).

**2 January 1844** - A metal **cockade** is established for the band on officers' forage caps, as introduced for officers' caps in regular forces (99).

**14 April 1845** - The batteries' previous jackets are replaced with a **chekmen**. Officers are ordered to wear **pistols** with cords only when in formation (100).

**27 April 1845** - Consequent to the **changes** in uniform of 14 April 1845 for the Orenburg Cossack artillery, there are established for its horse-artillery batteries:

Chekmen of dark-green cloth with a collar and cuffs of black cloth, with edging on the collar, cuffs, and down the front opening of red cloth; chekmen to reach to 4 vershoks [7 inches] above the knee. Headdress of black astrakhan 4-1/2 vershoks [7-7/8 inches] high, without an indentation, with a bag of scarlet cloth. Pistol case of the previous pattern but sewn into the holder and secured to the sword belt on the left side. All other items of uniform and weaponry, as well as horse furniture, not mentioned here remain unchanged (101).

**5 April 1849** - The batteries in the Orenburg Host's Horse-Artillery Brigade are ordered to have artillery draft **horses** of the Kirghiz steppe breed, no taller than 2 arshins 2 vershoks [59-1/2 inches] and no shorter than 1 arshin 15 vershoks [54-1/4 inches], from 5 to 7 years of age. They are to be branded after the manner in the Siberian Cossack Host on the croup so that the horses from these batteries, when with the Instructional platoon in St. Petersburg, are from domestic breeds as before (102).

**8 July 1852** - It is ordered that the **chekmen** be made after the example of chekmens in the Don and Caucasian Cossack artillery, with red edging down the front (103).

Apart from the changes in uniform described here for all units of the Orenburg Cossack Host, all orders promulgated in regard to the standard **general-officer's uniform** and the uniforms for **general-adjutants**, **aides-de-camp of H.I.M.**, and **adjutants** to Don Host generals, set forth above in the section for that Host, also apply to the Orenburg Cossack Host.

## VII. TEPTYAR REGIMENTS [*TEPTYARSKIE POLKI*].

**1 January 1827** - In order to differentiate between **ranks** in the 1st and 2nd Teptyar Regiments, small stamped stars are established for officers' epaulettes, as for regular forces (104).

**10 July 1827** - In these regiments it is ordered that there be round **pompons** on the headdress: white for lower ranks and silver for officers (105).

**15 November 1829** - These **regiments**, which have had dark-blue jackets with red piping on the collar and cuffs, red shoulder straps, and black sharovary pants with stripes, are ordered to have jackets with red piping also down the front, with light-blue shoulder straps on which is cut out the regimental number, on white cloth. Sharovary - dark-blue with the previous stripe. With this change lower ranks are prescribed standard cossack headdresses with a light-blue upper pompon, lower pompon, and bag; black girdles of a cotton material; boots with iron spurs; cavalry sabers as established for regular light cavalry regiments; black leather sword belts with brass buckles; pistols in a black leather holder worn on the left side, with a cord and tassel of light-blue mixed with black; small shiny black leather cartridge pouches [*podsumki*] with the a similar crossbelt without any metal fittings, and an iron ramrod on a black belt; carbines on a crossbelt of shiny black leather with metal fittins and an iron hook; lances with black shafts and a pennant of light blue with red. In mounted order saddlecloths of the usual cossack pattern made from dark-blue cloth with red trim. Later, on 3 May 1831, cloth saddle pillows were added after the manner of the L.-Gds. Cossack Regiments, and leather flaps [*tebenki*]; gray valises (Illus. 1247).

Officers were distinguished by the epaulettes prescribed for their ranks, sashes, and other silver appointments (Illus. 1248) (106).

The Teptyar regiments kept this uniform in its entirety up to their disbandment when they were used to form the **First Orenburg Cossack Regiment**, which took place in 1835 and is referred to above in the descriptions for regiments of the Orenburg Cossack Host.

## VIII. STAVROPOL KALMUCK HOST. [*STAVROPOL'SKOE KALMYTSKOE VOISKO.*]

**1 January 1827** - In order to differentiate between **ranks**, small stamped stars are established for officers' epaulettes, as for regular forces (107).

**10 July 1827** - In the Host it is ordered that there be round **pompons** on the headdress: white for lower ranks and silver for officers (108).

**15 November 1829** - This **Host**, which has had dark-blue jackets of standard cossack cut with a red collar and red piping on the cuffs and dark-blue sharovary pants with red stripes and piping is ordered to have jackets with collar, cuffs, and two shoulder straps (without a number), and sharovary with only a single red stripe. With this change lower ranks are prescribed standard cossack headdresses with a red bag and upper and lower pompons; red stamin girdles; boots without spurs. All other items are to be as for the Teptyar regiments, except for the pistol lanyard which is red with black, and the lance pennant whose upper half is black and lower half red (Illus. 1249).

As in other hosts, officers were distinguished by epaulettes, sashes, and the silver appointments prescribed for their rank (Illus. 1250) (109).

**20 January 1832** - Serving officers of the Host are allowed to wear silver **buttonhole loops** on collar and cuffs, after the example of the Ural and Orenburg Cossack Hosts (Illus. 1251) (110).

**15 July 1837** - Officers are given a new pattern **sash** with a narrow silver lace body with three stripes of light-orange and black silk, as established at this time for regular forces (111).

**17 December 1837** - An additional, fourth, thin twist of braid is added to officers' **epaulettes**, as in the regular forces (112).

**29 April 1838** - The **changes** in uniforms and weaponry promulgated on this date for regiments of the Astrakhan Cossack Host and described above apply in equal measure to the Stavropol Kalmuck Host, except for its prescribed distinctive colors (Illus. 1252). In this Host pennants are removed from the lances (113). Subsequently, nothing in the uniform, arms, or horse furniture of the Stavropol Kalmuck Host underwent any change up to the time of its disbandment and incorporation into the Orenburg Cossack Host, which took place on 24 May 1842.

## IX. BASHKIR-MESHCHERYAK HOST. [BASHKIRO-MESHCHERYAKSKOE VOISKO.]

**2 October 1829** - With the confirmation of uniform clothing for the **Bashkir-Meshcheryak Host**, its uniforms are to be according to the following description:

Cossacks of Bashkir cantons.

White cloth cap trimmed on the top seams with black tape and below with red colored cotton material. Black neckcloth of silk or any other material. Dark-blue cloth jacket of cossack style, closed with small hooks, with scarlet piping around the collar and cuffs. Scarlet shoulder straps with the cut-out number of the regiment on yellow cloth; white buttons for these straps. Dark-blue cloth sharovary pants of cossack pattern with single scarlet cloth stripe. Light-blue cotton girdle. Black boots.

Pistol on the left side in a black leather holster secured to the sword belt; for it a black cord with tassels. Small cartridge pouch [*podsumok*] of shiny black leather on a similar strap over the left shoulder, without fittings; on it an iron ramrod with a black strap wound around it. Carbine on a crossbelt of shiny black leather, with a brass buckle in back, slide, and endpiece, worn over the cartridge pouch; iron hook with spring. Black leather sword belt with two brass buckles. Saber in iron mountings of the pattern for all cavalry regiments. Lance on a black shaft, 4-1/2 arshins [10-1/2 feet] long (including the lance head) (Illus. 1253).

Non-commissioned officers [*uryadniki*] of Bashkir cantons.

On the coat the collar and cuffs are trimmed with silver galloon; white, black, and orange tassels on the cord; black caps (Illus. 1254).

Officers of Bashkir cantons.

Coats in all respects like those for lower ranks, but cartridge pouch on a black leather belt with silver fittings; sword belt likewise; black plissé headdress, trimmed with silver galloon with a black light; silver scaled epaulettes (Illus. 1255).

All ranks in Bashkir cantons.

Cossack saddle: saddlecloth of cossack style in dark-blue cloth, trimmed along the edges with scarlet cloth over the pad; valise of gray German cloth, secured along with the greatcoat behind the saddle; cossack bridle (Illus. 1253).

Cossacks of Meshcheryak cantons.

Black astrakhan headdress of the pattern for Don Cossacks, 4-1/2 vershoks [7-7/8 inches] high, top and bottom trimmed with black plissé, top of scarlet cloth with a bag hanging down the right side; pompon and cockade (lower pompon) of red wool; black leather chinstrap, one finger's breadth wide. Black silk neckcloth, or of any other material. Dark-blue cloth jacket of ccossack pattern, without piping, closed by small hooks. Shoulder straps of the same cloth with the cut-out number of the regiment on white cloth; white buttons on the straps. Dark-blue cloth sharovary pants of cossack style, with single stripes of scarlet cloth. Black cotton girdle. Black boots.

Pistol on the left side in a black leather holster secured to the sword belt; pistol lanyard with black wool tassels. Cartridge pouch of shiny black leather on a similar belt over the left shoulder, without fittings; iron ramrod wrapped in a black strap. Carbine on a black leather crossbelt with brass fittings behind, consisting of a buckle and endpiece; the crossbelt is worn over the left shoulder over the cartridge pouch; iron hook with spring. Black leather sword belt with two brass buckles. Saber in iron mountings of the pattern for all cavalry regiments. Lance with a black shaft 4-1/2 arshins [10-1/2 feet] long (including the lance head).

Non-commissioned officers of Meshcheryak cantons.

On the coat the collar and cuffs on the sleeves are trimmed with silver galloon; cockade (lower pompon) [*kokarda (repeek)*] under the upper pompon divided crosswise by dark-gray and white cloth; tassels on the cord colored white, black, and orange (Illus. 1256).

Officers of Meshcheryak cantons.

Uniform like that for lower ranks in all respects, but the cartridge pouch and sword belt have silver fittings; silver scaled epaulettes; silver pompon and cockade (lower pompon) (Illus. 1257).

All ranks in Meshcheryak cantons.

Cossack saddle: saddlecloth of cossack style in dark-blue cloth, trimmed along the edges with scarlet cloth over the pad; valise of gray German cloth, secured along with the greatcoat behind the saddle; bridle and all harness as for cossacks (114).

**15 July 1837** - Officers are given a new pattern **sash** with a narrow silver lace body with three stripes of light-orange and black silk, as established at this time for regular forces (115).

**17 December 1837** - An additional, fourth, thin twist of braid is added to officers' **epaulettes**, as in the regular forces (116).

**29 April 1838** - The **changes** in uniforms, weapons, and accouterments promulgated on this date for the Don, Black Sea, Astrakhan, Ural, and Orenburg Cossack Hosts, described above, are extended to the Bashkir-Meshcheryak Host, except for the Bashkirs' headdress, which remains unchanged (Illus. 1258 and 1295) (117).

**2 January 1844** - A metal **cockade** is established for the front of the band on officers' forage caps, as introduced at this time for officers' caps in regular forces (118).

**20 May 1844** - With the general allocation of colors for **forage caps** within the Military Administration, officers (Bashkir cantons as well as Meshcheryak) are to have caps as for Don Host officers: dark blue with a red band and red piping around the top (119).

**27 April 1845** - In the Bashkir-Meshcheryak Host are introduced the same **chekmens** and **pistol cases**, and additionally for Meshcheryak cantons—**headdress**, as established at this time for the Don Host and described above. The chekmens for officers in Bashkir cantons have buttonhole loops as before, while for officers in Meshcheryak cantons they are without buttonhole loops (Illus. 1260 and 1261) (120).

**12 February 1846** - It is established that:

1. In Bashkir and Meshcheryak cantons assigned a monetary payment in place of service, **no uniforms** or any kind of weapons are to be required, and they are allowed to wear their usual clothing.

2. When on cordon duty on the Orenburg Line, Bashkirs and Meshcheryaks in line cantons are allowed to wear their **national dress**, with uniform clothing required only if part of the host may be sent on external service toward the western or southern borders of the Empire (121).

## X. SIBERIAN LINE COSSACK HOST. [*SIBIRSKOE LINEINOE KAZACH'E VOISKO.*]

REGIMENTS

**1 January 1827** - In order to differentiate between **ranks**, small stamped stars are established for officers' epaulettes, as for regular forces (122).

**7 January 1829** - In place of their previous gold **epaulettes**, officers of the Siberian Line Cossack Host are to have silver scaled epaulettes. Instead of shakos, all ranks are to have the headdress prescribed for other cossack hosts (123).

**15 November 1829** - Regiments in the **Siberian Line Cossack Host** are prescribed the same uniforms, arms, and horse furniture as confirmed on this date for the Ural Cossack Host and described above, except with the light-blue color changed everywhere to red and the white numbers on the shoulder straps to yellow. The Siberian Line Cossack Host was further distinguished from other cossack hosts in that instead of a black chinstrap on the headdress, it had white metal **chinscales** (Illus. 1262 and 1263) (124).

**April 1831** - **Officers without permanent positions** [*zauryad-ofitsery*] are to have small stamped stars on their epaulettes, like those introduced on 1 January 1827 to distinguish rank (125).

**18 February 1837** - In the Siberian Line Cossack Host **bridles** [*uzdechki*] are established in place of curb-bits [*mundshtuki*], after the example of the L.-Gds. Cossack Regiment (126).

**15 July 1837** - Officers are given a new pattern **sash** of narrow silver lace with three stripes of light-orange and black silk, as for regular forces (127).

**17 December 1837** - Officers' **epaulettes** are given an additional fourth thin twist of braid (128).

**29 April 1838** - The **changes** in uniforms and weapons promulgated on this date for Don, Astrakhan, Ural, and Orenburg Cossack regiments, described above, are extended with equal force to the regiments of the Siberian Line Cossack Host, which in uniforms and arms, as well as horse furniture, is ordered to conform to the patterns for the cited regiments, except for its prescribed distinctions in colors. Along with this, the previous lance pennants in regiments of the Siberian Line Cossack Host are removed (Illus. 1264) (129).

**4 December 1840** - In the Siberian Line Cossack Host the dark-blue color of its uniforms is changed to **dark green**. Along with this, silver **buttonhole loops** are established for the collars and cuffs on officers' jackets, after the example of other cossack hosts (Illus. 1265) (130).

**2 January 1844** - A metal **cockade** is ordered to be worn on the band on officers' forage caps in the Orenburg Cossack Host, as established at this same time for officer' caps in regular forces (131).

**20 May 1844** - With the general allocation of colors for **forage caps** throughout the War Department, dark-green caps are established for the Siberian Lin Cossack Regiments, with a red band and red piping around the top (132).

**14 April 1845** - The current chekmens in the Siberian Line Cossack Host are replaced with **jackets** of the pattern established for Cossack generals when in Host uniform. Officers are ordered to wear pistols with cords only when in formation (133).

**27 April 1845** - As a consequence of the change on 14 April 1845 in the uniforms of the **Siberian Line Cossack Host**, the following uniform is established:

Dark-green chekmen, as before, but in length reaching to 4 vershoks [7 inches] above the knee, with a red edge on the collar and cuffs, and for officers the addition of their prescribed silver buttonhole loops; headdress of black fleece 4-1/2 vershoks [7-7/8 inches] high without an indentation on top, with a red cloth bag under which is sewn an oilcloth base; red girdle; pistol lanyard of the previous pattern but sewn to the carrier that is attached to the sword belt on the left side. The rest of the items of uniform clothing and weaponry, as well as horse furniture, remain unchanged (134).

**5 December 1846** - A description of the uniforms, weapons, and horse furniture for regiments of the **Siberian Line Cossack Host is confirmed**:

### Officers.

Headdress of black astrakhan with a red cloth crown and a chinstrap. Silver upper pompon. Silver lower pompon [repeek], lined with red cloth. Headdress cover of black lacquered oilcloth. Black silk neckcloth. Dark-green cloth chekmen with red piping around the collar and cuffs, closed with small hooks; silver buttonhole loops of cossack pattern on the collar and cuffs. Dark-green sharovary pants with red stripes. Red silk girdle. White suede gloves. Gray cloth greatcoat with red tabs on a dark-green collar piped red; smooth white metal buttons. Boots with iron spurs. Silver epaulettes with scales, with the regimental number, secured by a white metal button. Silver sash. Silver sword knot on a black leather strap. Forage cap of dark-green cloth with two lines of red piping, with a visor.

Ammunition pouch for 20 rounds in tin holders laid out in one row and lined with black morocco leather; trimmed on the bottom along the seam with thin black silk cord, with a black morocco lid trimmed along the edge with silver lace without a light. Ammunition pouch belt of silver lace without a light, lined with black morocco, 11/16 vershok [1-1/5 inches] wide, with silver buckles, slides, and endpieces. Carrier for stowing the pistol, of black morocco with two flaps, with stitching along the edges, 1-7/8 vershoks [3-1/4 inches] long on the left side, 3-1/2 [6-1/8] on the right; 3 vershoks [5-1/4 inches] wide at the top, 1-1/2 [2-5/8] at the bottom; silver pistol lanyard with one tassel and two slides, length 2 arshins 10 vershoks [73-1/2 inches]. Pistol case of dark-blue cloth to the lower part of the lock, then from the lower part of black morocco. Upwards, to the middle where the cloth ends, and below at the very bottom—trimmed around with silver lace without a light; for tying around the butt—a black silk cord; length of the case 7 vershoks [12-1/4 inches], 3-3/4 [6-1/2] wide at the top, 1-3/4 [3] wide in the middle, and 2 vershoks [3-1/2 inches] in circumference at the bottom; the lace 3-3/8 vershoks [5-9/10 inches] wide. Sword belt of the pattern established for light cavalry, modified so that the waist strap is whole and the slings sewn to it by means of an oval ring which is only half visible; trimmed with silver lace without a light.

Dark-blue cloth saddlecloth, trimmed along the edges with red tape 3/4 vershok [1-1/4 inches] wide. Saddle and harness of standard cossack style. Iron stirrups. Dark-green cloth pillow with red tape along the seams. Saddle-pad of sheepskin with a leather cover. Gray cloth valise. Bridle, harness, and chest-band [uzda, pafy i nagrudnik] of rawhide straps with iron fittings and bit. Shashka of the description confirmed on 29 April 1838. Light-cavalry pistol, worn in a carrier on the left side of the waist.

Adjutants of the Government Ataman and Host Duty Officer, as well as brigade adjutants, are prescribed a cossack pattern coat of dark-green cloth with a silver aiguilette; collar of red cloth; two silver buttonhole loops on the collar and cuffs, with brick-colored [bitogo tsveta] piping and girdle. Sharovary pants with red trim; cavalry saber.

### Cossacks.

Headdress as for officers. Red wool upper pompon. For cossacks the lower pompon is of red cloth, for non-commissioned officers of cloth striped across with dark gray and white. Cover of black oilcloth. Black cloth neckcloth. Dark-green cloth chekmen with red piping around the collar and cuffs. For trumpeters—with white tape trim after the pattern for regular troops. The collars and cuffs of non-commmissioned officers and staff-trumpeters are trimmed with silver galloon. Dark-green sharovary with red stripes. Red shalloon girdle. Gloves for non-commissioned officers and staff-trumpeters—suede; for cossacks and trumpeters—of dark-green cloth. Gray cloth greatcoat with red tabs on a dark-green collar, with red piping; smooth white metal buttons. Boots with iron spurs. Red cloth shoulder straps with a cut-out regimental number on yellow cloth, secured with a white metal button. Sword knot of red leather. Dark-green forage cap with two rows of red piping, without a visor.

Ammunition pouch for 40 rounds in tin holders laid in two rows, lined with black leather, with a lid of the same leather and stitching along the edges. Crossbelt for the ammunition pouch of black rawhide leather, 3/4 vershoks [1-1/4 inches] wide, with a brass buckle, slide, and endpiece. Carrier for stowing the pistol—of black leather with two side flaps, with stitching along the edges, 4 vershoks [7 inches] long on the left side and 5 [8-3/4] on the right, 4 vershoks [7 inches] wide at the top and 1-3/4 [3] at the bottom; pistol lanyard of red wool with one tassel and two slides, 2 arshins 7 veshoks [68-1/4 inches] long. Pistol case of dark-green cloth to the lower part of the lock, and from the bottom of shiny black leather; on top, in the middle, and toward the bottom trimmed with black tape; for tying around the butt - a red woolen cord with tassel; length of the cases 9-1/2 vershoks [16-5/8 inches], width at the top 3-1/2 [6-1/8] and at the bottom 1-3/4 [3]; below, the circumference of the bottom is 2-1/2 vershoks [4-3/8 inches]; tape on the cases is 1/4 vershok [1/2 inch] wide. Sword belt of shiny black leather with brass buckles; width of the strap - 6/8 vershok [1-1/4 inches].

Saddlecloth, saddle, cushion, sweat cloth, valise, bridle, harness, chest-band, shashka sword, and pistol—as for officers. Gray cloth saddle blanket.

Cossacks have dragoon muskets without a bayonet and a lance with a black shaft.

Host musicians have uniforms of the pattern for regimental lower ranks. For weapons they are only prescribed the shashka sword.

Reserve cossacks: forage cap - gray cloth with a dark-green band and two rows of red piping; visor, leather. Chekmen of gray cloth, dark-green collar with red piping and buttonhole loops; closed by small hooks. Red shoulder straps with the number of the regiment. Non-commissioned officers have silver galloon on the collar and cuffs. Gray sharovary with red piping. Black cloth neckcloth with a bib. Greatcoat - gray, with white tin buttons; gray collar with red piping and buttonhole loops. Shoulder straps as on the chekmen.

Carbine - of any pattern. Lance with a black shaft. Pistol of any pattern. Shashka or saber, ammunition pouch, sword belt, saddle, sweat cloth, stirrup straps - of the patterns established in the Host. Leather saddle pad. Bridle of rawhide straps. Iron curb-bit.

Noncombatant lower ranks in regiments and the Host administration in general—clerks, medical assistants, guards, bookbinders, printer, and draftsman: dark-green forage cap with the same band, red piping and a visor. Dark-green chekmen with red piping around the collar; closed with small hooks. Red shoulder straps with the regimental number. Silver galloon is sewn around the collar and cuffs of non-commissioned officers. Dark-green sharovary with red piping. Black cloth neckcloth with a bib. Gray greatcoat with a dark-green collar piped red; white buttons. Shoulder straps as on the chekmen.

Lower ranks in the Host craftsmen command and guards have uniforms as for reserve cossacks except for the girdle, which is not prescribed for them (135).

**14 April 1851** - In the Siberian Line Cossack Host, in place of the **lance buckets** of shiny leather prescribed by the equipment table of 5 December 1846 it is ordered to retain the rawhide leather straps already introduced in the Host (136).

**19 November 1851** - It is ordered that combatant non-commissioned officers of Siberian Line Cossack Host regiments be armed with **muskets**. All combatant lower ranks of these regiments are to have dragoon muskets with bayonets (137).

## ARTILLERY

(Changes in the numbering of artillery batteries in the Siberian Line Cossack Host are shown in Part I of Volume XIX, Chapter XXXIV of *Historical Description of the Clothing and Arms of the Russian Army.*)

**1 January 1827** - In order to differentiate between **ranks**, small stamped stars are established for officers' epaulettes, as for regular forces (138).

**7 August 1829** - Epaulettes with scaled fields are established for officers' uniforms, of the pattern for epaulettes in the regular light cavalry (139).

**15 November 1829** - The **artillery** of the Siberian Line Cossack Host receives the exact same uniforms, weapons, and horse furniture as used at this time in Don horse-artillery companies, with only the replacement of the black chinstrap on the headdress with brass **chinscales** (Illus. 1268) (140).

**15 July 1837** - Officers are given new pattern sashes with narrow silver lace with three stripes of light-orange and black silk, as for regular forces (141).

**17 December 1837** - To officers' **epaulettes** is added, following the example of the regular forces, a fourth thin twist of braid (142).

**29 April 1838** - The **changes** in uniforms and arms for Don Horse-Artillery batteries, described above, are applied in equal measure to the artillery of the Siberian Line Cossack Host (143).

**1 July 1839** - For lower ranks in **training detachments** of the Siberian Line Cossack Host horse artillery, the cadre of these detachments as well as the personnel rotated annually, there is ordered to have yellow tape around the epaulette, following the pattern confirmed for Instructional troops (144).

**2 January 1844** - A metal **cockade** is established for the band on officers' forage caps, as introduced for officers' caps in regular forces (145).

**14 April 1845** - The batteries' previous jackets are replaced with a **chekmen**. Officers are ordered to wear pistols with cords only when in formation (146).

**27 April 1845** - Consequent to the **changes** in uniform of 14 April 1845 for the Siberian Line Cossack artillery, there are established for its horse-artillery batteries:
Chekmen of dark-green cloth to reach to 4-1/2 vershoks [7-7/8 inches] above the knee, with collar and cuffs of black cloth, and red cloth edging on the collar, cuffs, and down the front opening. Headdress of black astrakhan 4-1/2 vershoks [7-7/8 inches] high, without an indentation, with a bag of scarlet cloth, under which is sewn an oilcloth base. Pistol case of the previous pattern but sewn into the holder and secured to the sword belt on the left side. All other items of uniform and weaponry, as well as horse furniture, remain unchanged (147).

**5 December 1846** - A description of the uniforms, weapons, and horse furniture for **Horse Artillery batteries** of the Siberian Host is confirmed:

**Officers.**

Headdress of black astrakhan with a red cloth crown and a chinstrap. Silver upper pompon. Silver lower pompon [*repeek*], lined with red cloth. Headdress cover of black lacquered oilcloth. Black silk neckcloth. Dark-green chekmen with black collar and cuffs, and red piping around the collar and cuffs. Dark-green sharovary pants with red stripes. Red silk girdle. White suede gloves. Gray cloth greatcoat with red tabs on a black collar piped red; brass buttons with artillery armature. Boots with iron spurs. Silver epaulettes with scales, with the battery number, secured by a button. Silver sash. Silver sword knot on a black leather strap. Forage cap of dark-green cloth with black band and three rows of piping, with a visor.
Ammunition pouch, pistol carrier, pistol lanyard, saddle, sweat-cloth, valise, shashka sword, and pis, saddle, sweat-cloth, valise, shashka sword, and pistol—of the patterns for Siberian Line Cossack Host regiments. Crossbelt for the ammunition pouch, pistol case, and sword belt—of the patterns for the regiments but with silver lace replaced by gold. Saddlecloth of dark-green cloth, trimmed along the edges with gold galloon piped red. Saddle cushion dark green with gold galloon. Bridle, harness, and chest-band of rawhide straps with brass fittings.

**Cossacks.**

Headdress, upper and lower pompons, headdress cover, and neckcloth—of the patterns established at this time for regimental cossacks in the Siberian Line Cossack Host. Chekmen the same as in the regiments, except for non-commissioned officers the collar and cuffs are trimmed with gold galloon. Dark-green sharovary with red stripes. Red shalloon girdle. White suede gloves. Raven's duck stable jacket [*kitel'*], with covered buttons. Gray greatcoat with red tabs on a black collar piped red; brass buttons with artillery armature. Boots with iron spurs. Brass epaulettes with scales, the battery number in white metal. Sword knot of red leather. Forage cap, ammunition pouch for 20 rounds, its crossbelt, pistol lanyard, pistol case, sword belt, saddle, sweat-cloth, valise, shashka, pistol, and saddle pad—of the patterns established at this time for regiments of the Siberian Line Cossack Host.
Dark-green cloth saddlecloth, trimmed along the edges with a yellow cloth stripe 3/4 vershok [1-1/4 inches] wide. Dark-green cushion with a yellow stripe along the seams. Bridle, harness, and chest-piece—of rawhide straps with brass fittings. Noncombatant lower ranks in the artillery brigade have uniforms of the pattern established by the table confirmed on 25 August 1816, supplemented by regulations, i.e. for non-commissioned officers—dark-green cloth forage caps and chekmens; for cossacks—gray cloth forage caps and jackets; for both—gray cloth riding trousers and greatcoats, and so on (148).

**8 June 1852** - It is ordered that **chekmens** in the Siberian Host's horse-artillery battery be made after the example of chekmens in the Don and Caucasian Cossack artillery, with red edging down the front (149).

Apart from the changes in uniform described here for all units of the Siberian Line Cossack Host, all orders promulgated in regard to the **standard general-officer's uniform** and the uniforms for **general-adjutants**, **aides-de-camp of H.I.M.**, and **adjutants** to Don Host generals, set forth above in the section for that Host, also apply to the Siberian Line Cossack Host.

## XI. SIBERIAN TOWN COSSACKS AND BORDER TROOPS [*SIBIRSKIE GORODOVYE KAZACH'YA I POGRANICHNYYA VOISKA*].

**15 January 1829** - All **Siberian town cossacks** and **border troops** are given uniform clothing of standard cossack style: jackets and chekmen - dark blue, with red collar and shoulder straps and tin buttons (on the shoulder straps). Gray sharovary pants with red piping. Dark-blue bag on the headdress, likewise dark-blue upper and lower pompons. Black girdle, black accouterments, dark-blue pistol lanyard, tassel, and saddlecloth, the saddlecloth with red trim (Illus. 1269 and 1270). Officers are prescribed silver epaulettes with scales and a red base, dark-blue girdles, cartridge pouches of shiny black leather and silver mountings, dark-blue saddlecloths with red trim, and other distinctions generally established for officers (Illus. 1271). Town regiments and border commands are ordere to be distinguished by Cyrillic letters and numerals (cut out on yellow cloth for lower ranks, of gilt metal for officers). In the Tobolsk Regiment - T. B., Siberian Tatar - S. T., Tomsk - Tm., Yeniseisk - Ye., Irkutsk - I., Trans-Baikal - Z., and Yakutsk - Ya.

In border commands under the Troitskosavsk administration: Tsurukhaituevsk - T. I., Kharatsaisk - T. III., and Tunkinsk - T. III. In other border commands following the same sequence, i.e. the letter T. joined with the numeral allocated to the command (150).

**17 December 1837** - A fourth, narrow, twist of braid is added to officers' **epaulettes**, after the example of regular forces (151).

**22 August 1840** - A description of the uniform and musket of the **Yakutsk Town Cossack Regiment** is confirmed; headdress of black lambskin, after the style for line cossacks; jacket of dark-green cloth with a red collar and red shoulder straps; dark-green cuffs; on the chest places for 10 cartridges, 5 on each side. Instead of a girdle a belt over the jacket, on which is a bayonet scabbard. Round pouch [*suma*] of cossack pattern, on the previous crossbelt, for 20 rounds. Sharovary pants of the same pattern (dark-gray cloth from Siberian factories); in the absence of this color then to be made in the St.-Petersburg commissariat from gray factory cloth. Infantry musket with jäger sling (Illus. 1272) (152).

**18 February 1842** - For noncombatant lower ranks of the **Yakutsk Town Cossack Regiment** the same uniform is established as prescribed on 22 August 1840 for its combatant personnel, but made from gray cloth and without weapons (Illus. 1273) (153).

**2 January 1844** - A metal **cockade** is established on the front of officers' forage cap bands, as for officers' caps in regular forces (154).

**21 October 1849** - Confirmation is given to a description of uniforms and arms:

**Tobolsk Cossack Foot Battalion.**

### Officers.

Headdress of red cloth, rounded top, quilted, trimmed around with wide silver lace and crossed with four strips of thin silver lace; brim of black sheepskin; chinstrap of black leather. Dark-green forage cap with a red band and red piping on top, with a visor. Black silk neckcloth. Dark-green chekmen with red collar and dark-green cuffs; closed with small hooks. The chekmen must be 5 vershoks [8-3/4 inches] higher than the knee. Silver epaulettes with the Cyrillic letters T. K. B. on a red field; secured by a white metal button. Silver sash. Waistbelt of silver lace backed with black morocco, with a silver buckle fastening in front. Dark-gray sharovary pants with red piping. Gray greatcoat with a collar of the same color with a red tab and red piping; white metal buttons, smooth. Boots without spurs. Shashka sword—according to the description confirmed on 29 April 1838. Cossack sword knot.

### Cossacks.

Headdress as for officers except white worsted tape instead of silver lace. Forage cap as for officers but without a visor. Black cloth neckcloth. Chekmen as for officers. For non-commissioned officers the collar and cuffs have the usual silver army galloon. For hornists the chest, sleeves, back, and shoulder wings are trimmed with white tape as in regular forces. Red cloth shoulder straps with the letters T. K. B. cut out on yellow cloth. Waistbelt of shiny black leather 6/8 vershok [1-1/4 inches] wide; fastened in front with a single buckle; bayonet scabbard secured to the waistbelt. Cartridge pouch [*podsumok*] of black Russian leather, for 20 rounds; worn at the waist by means of leather straps in such a manner that it may be freely moved all around the waist. (Hornists are not authorized.) Dark-gray sharovary with red piping. Soldier pattern greatcoat, gray, with a similarly colored collar with red tabs; white metal buttons, smooth.

The musket for cossacks and non-commissioned officers is the infantry pattern with a bayonet. The sling, lock cover, and flint case are as for infantry. Knapsack of calf leather, closed with three iron buckles; on a black crossbelt of black Russian leather 3/4 vershok [1-1/4 inches] wide, worn over the right shoulder after the example of Black Sea foot cossack battalions.

Noncombatant ranks - clerks, medical assistants, and barbers are prescribed a forage cap, chekmen, sharovary, neckcloth, and greatcoat of the battalion pattern.

### Tobolsk Horse Cossack Regiment.

Officers.

Headdress of red cloth, rounded top, quilted, trimmed around with wide silver lace and crossed with four strips of thin silver lace; brim of black sheepskin; chinstrap of black leather. Dark-green forage cap with a red band and red piping on top, with a visor. Black silk neckcloth. Dark-green chekmen with red collar and dark-green cuffs; closed with small hooks. The chekmen must be 5 vershoks [8-3/4 inches] higher than the knee. Dark-gray sharovary pants with leather reinforcements [kozhanya stremyanki] and red piping. Dark-green silk girdle. Silver epaulettes with scales, of the confirmed pattern, secured with a white metal button, with the Cyrillic letters T. K. P. Silver sash. Cavalry sword knot. Sword belt of silver lace without a light, backed with black morocco.

Ammunition pouch of black morocco with a similar lid, for 20 rounds. Pistol carrier of black morocco with two side flaps, stitched along the sides, 1-7/8 [3-1/4 inches] vershoks long on the left side and 3-1/2 [6-1/8] on the right, 3 vershoks [5-1/4 inches] wide at the top, 1-1/2 [2-5/8] below. Silver pistol lanyard, with one tassel and two slides, 2 arshins 10 vershoks [73-1/2 inches] long.

Saddlecloth of dark-green cloth, trimmed along the edges with a red stripe 3/4 vershok [1-1/4 inches] wide. Saddle of cossack pattern, with iron stirrups. Saddle pad of black leather, with the same piping. Sweat-cloth of sheep's wool with leather cover. Gray cloth valise. Bridle with two reins and brass fittings.

Shashka sword—according to the description confirmed on 29 April 1838. Cavalry pistol, worn in a carrier at the left side of the waist.

Cossacks.

Headdress as for officers except with white worsted tape. Forage cap as for officers but without a visor. Black cloth neckcloth. Chekmen as for officers. For non-commissioned officers the collar and cuffs have the usual silver galloon. Sharovary as for officers. Dark-green girdle of shalloon. Gloves for non-commissioned officers—white suede, for cossacks—dark-green cloth. Greatcoat as in the infantry battalion. Boots with iron spurs. Red shoulder straps with the Cyrillic letters T.K.P. cut out on yellow cloth. Sword belt of black rawhide leather.

Ammunition pouch [patrontash] of black Russian leather with a similar lid, for 20 rounds. Pistol carrier of black leather with two flaps, with stitching along the sides, 4 vershoks [7 inches] long on the left side and 5 [8-3/4] on the right, 4 vershoks wide at the top and 1-3/4 [3 inches] wide at the bottom. pistol lanyard of red wool, with a tassel and two slides, 2 arshins 7 vershoks [68-1/4 inches] long.

Saddlecloth, saddle, cushion, sweat-cloth, valise, shashka, and pistol—as for officers. Bridle with halter and no fittings. Lance with a black shaft and iron spearhead and endpiece.

Noncombatant ranks - clerks and medical assistants are prescribed forage caps, chekmen, sharovary, neckcloth, and greatcoat of the regimental patterns (155).

**4 January 1851** - Confirmation is given to a description of uniforms and weapons for the **Irkutsk** and **Yeniseisk Cossack Horse Regiments**.

Officers.

Headdress of red cloth, rounded top, quilted, trimmed around with wide silver lace and crossed with four strips of thin silver lace; brim of black sheepskin; chinstrap of black leather. Dark-green forage cap with a red band and red piping on top, with a visor. Black silk neckcloth. Dark-green chekmen with red collar and dark-green cuffs; closed with small hooks. The chekmen must be 5 vershoks [8-3/4 inches] higher than the knee. Black velvet cartridge-holder [napatronnik], with internal pockets, trimmed around with wide silver lace; tube of Karelian birch with silvered caps; each cartridge-holder for 8 rounds. Gray sharovary pants with leather reinforcements [kozhanya stremyanki] and red piping. Waistbelt of silver lace 6/8 vershok [1-1/4 inches] wide, backed with black morocco, with double and small buckles, endpiece, and slide. White suede gloves. Gray greatcoat with similarly colored collar with red tabs; white buttons, metal, smooth. Boots with iron spurs. Silver epaulettes with scales, with the Cyrillic letters I. P. for the Irkutsk Regiment and Ye. P. for the Yeniseisk. Cavalry sword knot. Sword belt of silver lace without a light, backed with black morocco.

Cavalry pistol, worn at the left side of the waist. Pistol carrier of black morocco with two side flaps, stitching along the sides, 1-7/8 [3-1/4 inches] vershoks long on the left side and 3-1/2 [6-1/8] on the right, 3 vershoks [5-1/4 inches] wide at the top, 1-1/2 [2-5/8] below. Silver pistol lanyard with one tassel and two slides, 2 arshins 10 vershoks [73-1/2 inches] long. Shashka sword according to the description confirmed on 29 April 1838.

The saddle consists of a tree, girth, stirrup straps with stirrups, sweat-cloth, crupper, surcingle, and cover with cushion. Cover and cushion of black leather, trimmed along the edges with red morocco and silver galloon. Bridle of rawhide leather, with brass fittings. Halter made from a rawhide strap. Cossack nagaika whip.

**Cossacks.**

Headdress as for officers except with white worsted tape instead of sliver lace. Forage cap as for officers but without a visor. Black cloth neckcloth. Chekmen as for officers. For non-commissioned officers the collar and cuffs are trimmed with silver galloon. Black leather cartridge-holder with internal pockets, trimmed with black tap and black cord; birch tubes with white bone caps, each cartridge-holder for 8 rounds. Sharovary as for officers. Waistbelt of black leather 6/8 vershoks [1-1/4 inches] wide, with iron fittings. Suede gloves for non-commissioned officers, and for cossacks—of dark-green cloth. Soldier pattern greatcoat, gray, with an identically colored collar with red tabs; white metal buttons, smooth. Boots with iron spurs. Red cloth shoulder straps with the Cyrillic letters I.P and Ye.P. cut out on yellow cloth. Black sword belt. of rawhide leather, worn over the shoulder.

Ammunition pouch [*patrontash*] of black Russian leather with a similar lid, for 40 rounds, of the pattern for His Royal Highness the Crown Prince of Württemberg's Dragoon Regiment. Its crossbelt—of black rawhide leather 6/8 vershoks wide.

Infantry musket with bayonet, which is worn in a scabbard on the shashka sword. Musket sling and shashka—according to the description confirmed on 29 April 1838. Case for musket—of leather prepared with the hair side outwards. Iron lance head on a black shaft. Saddle as for officers but without galloon trim. Bridle with halter tie-rope and no fittings. Halter and nagaika whip as for officers.

Clerks and medical assistants are prescribed forage caps, chekmen, sharovary, neckcloth, and greatcoat of the regimental patterns (156).

**17 March 1851** - Uniforms and weapons are confirmed for the **Russian mounted regiments** of the **Trans-Baikal Cossack Host**, in all respects completely like those for the Irkutsk and Yeniseisk regiments, with the only difference being that on officers' epaulettes and lower ranks' shoulder straps there is the regimental number and the Cyrillic letter Z (157).

**21 July 1851** - Confirmation is given to a description of uniforms and weapons for **foot battalions** of the **Trans-Baikal Cossack Host**.

Officers.

Headdress of dark-green cloth, rounded top, quilted, trimmed aroundwith wide silver lace and crossed with four strips of thin silver lace; fur brim; chinstrap of black leather. Dark-green forage cap with red piping on top, with a visor. Black silk neckcloth. Dark-green chekmen with a red piping on the collar and cuffs; closed with small hooks. The chekmen must be 5 vershoks [8-3/4 inches] higher than the knee. Silver epaulettes on a red field, with the battalion number, secured with a white metal button. Sword belt of silver lace 6/8 vershok [1-1/4 inches] wide, backed with black morocco, with silver double and small buckles, endpiece, and slides. Gray sharovary pants without piping.

Officer pattern greatcoat, gary, with a collar of the same color piped red; white metal buttons, smooth. Boots without spurs. Shashka sword according to the description confirmed 29 April 1838. Infantry sword knot. Sword belt over the shoulder, of silver lace without a light, backed with black morocco with silver fittings.

Cavalry pistol. Pistol carrier of black morocco, worn behind at the waist. Dark-green cloth case. Silver cord.

Cossacks.

Headdress as for officers except with white worsted tape instead of silver lace. Forage cap without a visor. Black cloth neckcloth. Chekmen as for officers. For non-commissioned officers the collar and cuffs are trimmed with silver army galloon. For drummers the breast, sleeves, back, and shoulder wings are trimmed with white tape as in regular forces. Dark-green shoulder straps with red piping and the battalion number on yellow cloth. Waistbelt and sharovary as for officers, but the waistbelt with iron fittings. Soldier pattern greatcoat, gray, with a collar of the same color piped red, with a white metal button. For winter a half-length fur coat [*polushubok*] over the chekmen.

Musket—infantry pattern for cossacks and non-commissioned officers, with bayonet; bayonet scabbard hung from the waistbelt as in Black Sea Cossack battalions. Musket sling, lock cover, and flint case of infantry patterns. For cossacks and non-commissioned officers a ammunition pouch of black Russian leather for 40 rounds, after the pattern for Black Sea foot battalions; crossbelt of black rawhide 6/8 vershok [1-1/4 inches] wide. Knapsack of calf-skin, closed with three iron buckles, on a black crossbelt of rawhide leather 3/4 vershok [1-1/4 inches] wide, worn over the right shoulder as in Black Sea Cossack battalions. Standard cavalry pistol (for drummers); its carrier of black Russian leather, worn behind at the waist; dark-green cloth case; black worsted cord.

Noncombatant lower ranks are prescribed a forage cap, chekmen, sharovary, neckcloth, and greatcoat of the patterns established for the battalion (158).

**6 March 1852** - Changes are confirmed for the uniforms of personnel in the Tobolsk Foot Cossack Battalion and Tobolsk Horse Cossack Regiment (Illus. 1274).

**Tobolsk Foot Cossack Battalion**.

Headdress (for lower ranks)—the top trimmed with thread tape [*nityanaya tes'ma*] instead of worsted. Chekmen (for officers and lower ranks), red piping of chancellery cloth [*kantselyarskoe sukno*] around the top of the cuffs. Waistbelt (for lower ranks) closed by a black iron plate buckle, as in Caucasus forces. Cartridge pouch [*podsumok*] (for lower ranks) replaced by ammunition pouch [*patrontash*] for 40 rounds (of the pattern confirmed for the Caucasus Sapper and Rifle battalions); ammunition pouch worn over the left shoulder on a strap of Russian leather polished black; strap 6/8 ver-shok [1-1/4 inches] wide.

In the case of the battalion being armed with percussion muskets, then a firing-cap pouch will be sewn to the ammu-nition pouch under the lid, as in the Caucasus forces. Knapsack (for lower ranks)—worn on two straps: the straps of Russian leather polished black, 1 vershok [1-3/4 inches] wide, worn crosswise over the chest, as in Black Sea Cossack battalions. To the knapsack is secured: for men of the 1st and 3rd ranks—mess tins; for the middle rank—kettles. The greatcoat is rolled on top of the knapsack in the infantry manner. Straps for securing the mess tins and kettles, as well as greatcoats, are to be of the same leather as the knapsack straps; the mess-tin strap 1/2 vershok [7/8 inches] wide, and that for the kettle 3/4 vershok [1-1/4 inches].

In the case of the battalion being armed with percussion muskets, a slit flap for a small iron case for spare firing caps will be made under the top flap of the knapsack.

### Tobolsk Horse Cossack Regiment.

Headdress (for lower ranks)—thread tape on top instead of worsted. Chekmen with red piping along the top of the cuffs. In the case of the regiment being armed with percussion muskets, then a firing-cap pouch will be sewn to the ammuni-tion pouch under the lid, as in the Caucasus forces (159).

**6 August 1853** - Changes are confirmed in the previous descriptions of arms and uniforms of the Irkutsk and Yeniseisk Horse Cossack Regiments, and also the horse regiments and foot battalions of the Trans-Baikal Cossack Host.

### Irkutsk and Yeniseisk Horse Cossack Regiments (Illus. 1275).

### Officers.

Headdress of red cloth, rounded top, quilted, height from the brim 2 vershoks [3-1/2 inches], trimmed around with wide silver lace and crossed with four strips of thin silver lace Brim of black sheepskin; its width including the wool 3 vershoks [5-1/4 inches]; chinstrap of black Russian leather 1/2 vershok [7/8 inch] wide, fastened with a small hook. Forage cap and neckcloth as before. Dark-green cloth chekmen with red collar and dark-green cuffs, with red piping on the cuffs, closed with small hooks; rear skirts at the back folded in pleats [*slozheny sborkami*]; collar lined with dark-green cloth; skirts to 5 vershoks [8-3/4 inches] above the knee.

Black velvet cartridge holder with internal pockets trimmed around with wide silver lace; tubes of Karelian birch with silvered caps; each cartridge holder for 8 rounds; a silver cord is passed through the caps and fastened with a hook to a small silvered plate that is secured by this hook to a thread buttonhole loop on the breast. Sharovary—of gray cloth with red piping, with pockets; instead of one strap on the lower legs leather footstraps are sewn, with two bone toggles for fastening, after the manner of cavalry riding trousers.

Waistbelt, gloves, greatcoat, boots, epaulettes, sword knots, pistol, pistol lanyard, shashka, saddle, bridle, and halter are left as before. Sword belt of silver lace without a light, backed with black morocco, with silver fittings, worn over the shoulder. Holder for stowing the pistol—of black morocco with two side flaps and edging of black morocco, 1-7/8 [3-1/4 inches] vershoks long on the left side and 3-1/2 [6-1/8] on the right, 3 vershoks [5-1/4 inches] wide at the top, 1-1/2 [2-5/8] below, with a leather tube 4 vershoks [7 inches] long and, sewn to the tube, dark-green cloth 5 vershoks [8-3/4 inches] long, with a silver cord 9-1/2 vershoks [16-5/8 inches] long, with tassels like those for cossack officers.

Plaited nagaika whip made from a rawhide strap, 9 vershoks [15-3/4 inches] long, with a rawhide tip and wooden handle 7 vershoks [12-1/4 inches] long; 1 vershok [1-3/4 inches] from the end of the handle a rawhide strap is passed.

### Cossacks.

Headdress of red chancellery cloth with a canvas lining; for non-commissioned officers the top is trimmed around with white thread tape 1/2 vershok [7/8 inch] wide, and with narrow tape 1/4 vershok [1/2 inch] wide laid crosswise; for cossacks only the crosswise narrow tape. Brim as for officers; chinstrap of black Russian leather, 1/2 vershok [7/8 inch] wide; on the chinstrap's right side is sewn a similar leather toggle, and a slit is cut on the left. Forage cap and neckcloth remain unchanged. The previous chekmen: linen lining sewn in from the collar to the waist; rank insignia in white tape sewn onto the shoulder straps. Black leather cartridge holder, with internal pockets, trimmed around with black tape 1/4 vershok [1/2 inch] wide at the bottom and 1/2 [7/8] at the top; similar wide tape is sewn around the cloth; birch tubes with white bone caps; each cartridge holder to fit 8 rounds. Through the caps is passed a black cord that is fastened with small hooks to a brass-tin [*mednoluzhennaya*] plate. The plate is secured to the breast with a thread buttonhole loop. Sharovary as for officers, of gray army cloth, lined with linen; under the waist and 2-1/2 vershoks [4-3/8 inches] below to the right is sewn a pocket of the same linen lining. Waistbelt, gloves, and boots are unchanged. Soldier pattern greatcoat, of gray cloth, collar of the same with red tabs; red cloth shoulder straps with the Cyrillic letters I. P. or Ye. P. cut through and backed with yellow cloth. Tabs on the greatcoat collar, rear cinches, and front opening as in the cavalry; tin buttons, smooth. Rank insignia of white tape. The greatcoat must be 4 vershoks [7 inches] from the ground. Sword belt of black rawhide leather, 1/2 vershok [7/8 inch] wide, with iron fittings, two rings, three buckles, and an endpiece, passed through an iron slide; sword belt worn of the shoulder.

Pistol as for officers, authorized only for non-commissioned officers and trumpeters. Holder of shiny black leather with two flaps and edging of black leather, 4 vershoks [7 inches] long on the left side and 5 [8-3/4] on the right, 4 vershoks wide at the top and 1-3/4 [3 inches] wide at the bottom, with a leather tube 4 vershoks [7 inches] long, and sewn to it dark-green cloth 5 vershoks [8-3/4 inches] long; cord of red wool, 2 arshins 7 vershoks [68-1/4 inches] long; for non-commissioned officers with a multicolored tassel and two similarly colored, for cossacks with a red tassel and a similar slide. Ammunition pouch of black Russian leather with a similar lid, for 40 rounds. In the Irkutsk Regiment with tin tubes and in the Yeniseisk Regiment with iron, after the pattern for His Royal Highness the Crown Prince of Württemberg's Dragoon Regiment. Shashka sword as for officers; two brass rings are affixed to it to hang the bayonet scabbard, after the manner for dragoon shashkas.

Infantry musket with bayonet, the latter worn in a scabbard on the shashka; small bracket for the sling positioned as on dragoon muskets so that it may be worn behind the back when in mounted order. Musket case of calfskin leather with the hair outwards, lined inside with gray cloth; a slit is made underneath to allow the musket to be inserted, edged with leather. For 12 vershoks [21 inches] along the slit is sewn a slide 1/4 vershok [1/2 inch] wide, through which passes a strap for fastening to a brass buckle sewn to a second slide 8-1/2 vershoks [15 inches] from the first, 1 arshin 6 vershoks [38-1/2 inches long and 3/4 [1-1/4] wide; 6 vershoks [10-1/2 inches] inside the slit, where the musket lock would lie, black leather is sewn onto the gray cloth for 4-1/2 vershoks [7-7/8 inches], so that the cloth does not wear through; on this same cloth is also sewn a leather toggle with a small loop for closing the slit. Lance, saddle, bridle, and halter—as before. Nagaika as for officers.

**Foot battalions of the Trans-Baikal Cossack Host** (Illus. 1276).

**Officers.**

Headdress of dark-green cloth, round at the top, quilted, trimmed around with wide silver lace and with four narrow strips of lace laid crosswise, also silver; brim of black dog hair, or other type of fur more easily found where the host is located; chinstrap of black leather 1/2 vershok [7/8 inch] wide. Dark-green forage cap, with two lines of piping around the top and above the band, with a visor. Dark-green chekmen with red piping along the collar and cuffs, closed with small hooks; 4 pleats behind and at the sides, on each side, with pockets between the pleats; skirts to 5 vershoks [8-3/4 inches] of the knee. Black velvet cartridge holder on the chest, trimmed around with wide silver lace, and on the black morocco bottom with narrow silver lace; holders for 6 cartridges on each side of the chest, of Karlian birch in silver mountings, with the same chains to fasten to the chekmen as for Black Sea foot cossack battalions. Neckcloth, epaulettes, and waistbelt—as before. Gray sharovary without piping, with two pockets. Summer sharovary of fine white linen, with a sewn-on belt of the same and two pockets, in all respects similar to the winter sharovary. Greatcoat as before. Army infantry boots.

Shashka, sword knot, and sword belt—as before.

Cavalry pistol. Holder of black morocco, worn at the waist on the left side, next to the shashka. Case with an upper part of dark-green cloth; trimmed around the closure with narrow silver lace; the lower part of black morocco; trimmed with the same lace where the leather joins the cloth and at one end; closed with a black silk cord with tassel. Silver pistol lanyard.

**Cossacks.**

Headdress as for officers. For non-commissioned officers the top is trimmed around with white thread tape, and has the same tape but narrow, only 1/4 vershok [1/2 inch] wide, laid crosswise; for cossacks only the crosswise narrow tape. For the detachment with the Instructional Regiment the brim is made of black sheep's fleece. The forage cap is as for officers but without a visor. Chekmen as for officers: the collar and body of the chekmen lined with linen down to the waist; for non-commissioned officers the collar and cuffs are trimmed with silver army infantry galloon; dark-green cloth shoulder straps with red piping and the battalion number cut out on yellow cloth. Neckcloth, waistbelt, and boots—as before. Winter sharovary gray, without piping, lined with linen; summer sharovary of army Flemish linen, with the same sewn-on waistbelt and two pockets made from linen. Soldier pattern greatcoat, of gray cloth, a collar of the same, dark-green cloth shoulder straps with the battalion number on yellow cloth; collar and shoulder straps with piping of red crepe cloth; collar lined with linen, the shoulder straps with gray cloth; smooth tin buttons.

Infantry musket with bayonet, also prescribed for non-commissioned officers; bayonet scabbard hung on the waistbelt, after the manner of Black Sea Cossack battalions. Musket sling and flint case—of Russian leather polished black, after the example of regular troops. Lock cover—as for infantry. Ammunition pouch of black Russian leather, with spaces for 40 rounds, of the pattern for Caucasus sappers; worn over the left shoulder on a crossbelt of white Russian leather under black polish, 6/8 vershok [1-1/4 inch] wide.

Infantry knapsack of calfskin with straps of Russian leather polished black, 1 vershok [1-3/4 inch] wide, worn crosswise on the chest after the manner of Tobolsk cossacks. An iron pot it secured to the knapsack, and on top a greatcoat rolled in the infantry fashion, also as for Tobolsk cossack; the straps for securing pots and greatcoats are made from the same leather as for knapsack straps; pot straps are 1/2 vershok [7/8 inch] wide, greatcoats straps 3/4 [1-1/4].

Drummers: headdress, forage cap, neckcloth, waistbelt, winter and summer sharovary, greatcoat, boots, and knapsack—as for cossacks. Chekmen—the same, but trimmed with white army tape, without a light, on the breast, sleeves, and shoulder wings of musicians of non-commissioned officer rank, and along the back seams, as for Black Sea Cossack battalions. Cartridge-holder on the chest of black leather, trimmed around with wide dark-green worsted tape; the bottom with narrow tape. The cartridge-holders on each side of the chest are for 6 rounds of white tin attached to black cords passed through an identical cord secured to the chekmen, in the same way as for Black Sea Cossack battalions. Drummer's crossbelt—of white Russian leather under black polish, of the pattern for jäger regiments, 2-1/2 vershoks [4-3/4 inches] wide. Pistol—cavalry pattern. Carrier—of shiny black leather, the same pattern as for Black Sea Cossack battalions, worn at the waist between the knapsack and left thigh, with the butt turned under the left hand. Pistol case—the upper part of dark-green army cloth lined with canvas, at the closure trimmed with narrow dark-green worsted tape; the lower part of shiny black leather; trimmed with the same tape where the cloth and leather join; closed with a black worsted cord with tassel. pistol lanyard—black worsted.

**Russian horse regiments of the Trans-Baikal Host** (Illus. 1277).

**Officers.**

Headdress of red cloth, round at the top, quilted, 2 vershoks [3-1/2 inches] high from the brim, trimmed around with wide silver lace and crossed with four strips of narrow silver lace; brim of black dog hair or other type of fur, 3 vershoks [5-1/4 inches] wide; chinstrap of black Russian leather 1/2 vershok [7/8 inch] wide, fastened with a small hook. Dark-green cloth chekmen, with red collar and dark-green cuffs, red piping on the cuffs; closed with small hooks down to the waist; folded pleats behind on the skirts; collar lined with dark-green cloth; skirts to 5 vershoks [8-3/4 inches] of the knees.

Cartridge-holder of black velvet, with internal pockets, trimmed around with wide silver lace; tubes of Karelian birch, with silvered caps; each cartridge-holder for 8 rounds; a silver cord is passed through the caps, as in the Irkutsk and Yeniseisk Horse Regiments.

Gray sharovary with red piping and pockets; instead of one strap on the lower legs leather footstraps are sewn, with two bone toggles for fastening, after the manner of cavalry riding trousers. Forage cap, neckcloth, waistbelt, gloves, greatcoat, boots, epaulettes, sword knot, sword belt, pistol, cord, shashka, saddle, bridle, and halter—remain unchanged. Nagaika and carrier for stowing the pistol—of the patterns established for the Irkutsk and Yeniseisk regiments.

**Cossacks.**

Headdress as for officers; for non-commissioned officers the top is trimmed around with white thread tape 1/2 vershok [7/8 inch] wide, and with narrow tape 1/4 vershok [1/2 inch] wide laid crosswise; for cossacks only the crosswise narrow tape; chinstrap of black Russian leather 1/2 vershok [7/8 inch] wide; on the chinstrap's right side is sewn a similar leather toggle, and a slit is cut on the left. Chekmen of the same pattern as for officers; from the collar down to the waist lined with linen; for non-commissioned officers the collar and cuffs are trimmed with silver cavalry galloon; shoulder straps of light-blue army cloth with the regimental number cut out on yellow cloth; rank distinctions of white tape.

Forage cap, neckcloth, waistbelt, gloves, boots, pistol, ammunition pouch, crossbelt, musket, lance, saddle, bridle, and halter—remain unchanged.

Cartridge-holder on the chekmen, sharovary pants, sword belt, holder for stowing the pistol, cord, musket case, and nagaika whip—of the patterns established for the Irkutsk and Yeniseisk regiments.

Greatcoat—of soldier pattern, gray cloth, with a collar of the same with red tabs; shoulder straps of light-blue army cloth with the regimental number cut out on yellow cloth. Tabs on the greatcoat collar, rear cinches, and front opening as in the cavalry; smooth tin buttons. Rank insignia of white tape, according to pattern. The greatcoat must reach to 4 vershoks [7 inches] from the ground (160).

**6 January 1854** - Confirmation is given to a description of **saddles** and full horse furniture for Russian horse regiments of the **Trans-Baikal Cossack Host**.

The saddle consists of an saddle-tree, girth, stirrup straps with stirrups, chestband, crupper, sweat-cloth, and cases with cushion. The arch is standard cossack style, the upper part with black leather and glue; both sides are fastened to two straps to which the chestband and girth attatch. Girth 1 arshin 9 vershoks [43-3/4 inches] long, 1-1/8 vershok [2 inches] wide; iron buckles are sewn to it from both sides. The second girth, or outer surcingle, is of the same width but 2-3/4 arshins [77 inches] long, so that it goes entirely around the horse through the saddle. The stirrup straps hang from the arch on both sides in front of the surcingle; they are rawhide straps, doubled over, with iron buckles, 2-1/2 arshins [70 inches] long and 1-1/4 [2-3/16 wide, onto which are fastened the iron stirrups. At both the front and rear arches of the tree are affixed three narrow rawhide straps with iron buckles for securing the full campaign load. The chestband is of normal cossack straps 7/8 vershok [1-1/2 inches] wide. Standard cossack crupper, 7/8 vershok wide.

The sweat-cloth is of standard cossack style made of wool felt, with a leather cover; 15 vershoks [26-1/4 inches] long in the center, 13-1/2 [23-1/4] wide in front and 1 arshin 2-1/2 vershoks [32-1/2 inches] at the rear; the lower 2 layers in front are trimmed with leather, and the upper two layers are sewn to the end of the leather cover, on each side of which is a shiny leather slide through which to pass load straps.

Case to cover the saddle-tree—of black calfskin, made from two halves; the middle seam sewn with leather; the edges of the top part trimmed with red morocco stripes 1 vershok [1-3/4 inches] wide, and for officers—additionally with silver galloon. Openings are made through which to pass load straps: 3 in the front and 3 in the rear, and 2 on the sides for the stirrup straps. The case is 1 arshin [28 inches] wide in front, 1 arshin 2-1/2 vershoks [32-1/2 inches] at the back, and 1 arshin long.

Cushion of black calfskin leather, sewn from two halves, sewn around with red morocco stripes and edges, and for officers—also with silver galloon. All four corners are rounded. The cushion is 9-1/2 vershoks [16-5/8 inches] long in the middle, 8 [14] wide in front, and 10 [17-1/2] wide in the rear. In the middle of the cushion is an opening with a tab; the tab is 6-3/4 vershoks [11-1/8 inches] long and 1 [1-3/4] wide; on the tab are punched 6 small holes for securing a small rawhide strap.

Bridle—normal cossack style, of rawhide leather, with brass fittings for officers, for cossacks with buckles and iron bit without fittings.

Valise—of gray cloth, after the patten for the Tobolsk Horse Cossack Regiment. In a cossack valise there are stowed, starting from the right side: smock, 2 shirts, wool socks, neckcloth, earmuffs, linen pants. From the left side: sharovary, foot wraps, rusk sack, and bag for groats and salt (161).

**19 March 1854** - In a supplement to the confirmed description of uniforms for horse regiments of the **Trans-Baikal Cossack Host**, announced in an order from the Minister of War on 6 August 1853, the **trumpeters** of these regiments are ordered to have: chekmen trimmed with white tape, as is general for trumpeters in cossack hosts; cartridge-holders on the breast according to the pattern confirmed for regiments of the Trans-Baikal Host (each of 8 wooden tubes with bone caps, through which passes a worsted cord from underneath the small plate); pockets for the tubes are trimmed with four rows of white tape, of which the last row goes along the bottom of the pockets; under the pockets and along the sides there is the same tape. The cartridge-holder is to be sewn onto the breast in a straight line, 2-1/2 vershoks 4-1/2 inches] from the collar down the front opening, from the opening to the tubes at the top 1-1/8 [2], at the bottom 3/4 [1-1/4], andfrom the front end of the shoulder wing to the cartridge-holder's tape 1 [1-3/4]. Signal trumpets are made in the same tone as brass light cavalry trumpets, 8-1/2 vershoks [14-7/8 inches] long including the mouthpiece, wrapped with four-sided white cord (as is general in the cavalry), with similar tassels. For staff-trumpeters and non-commissioned officer trumpeters the tassels have orange and black lights (162).

# NOTES

(1) Collection of Laws and Directives relating to the Military Administration [*Sobranie zakonov i postanovlenii, do chasti voennago upravleniya otnosyashchikhsya*], Book I, pg. 3.

(2) Ibid. 1829, Book III, pg. 127.

(3) Information received from the War Department's Commissariat Department, and confirmed patterns preserved there.

(4) Collection of Laws and Directives relating to the Military Administration, 1831, Book II, pg. 33.

(5) Information received from the War Department's Commissariat Department, and confirmed patterns preserved there.

(6) Collection of Laws and Directives, 1836, Book III, pg. 219.

(7) Order of the Minister of War, 1843, No. 44.

(8) Memorandum of the Minister of War to the Commander-in-Chief of the Separate Caucasus Corps, 2 October 1843, No. 1066.

(9) Confirmed patterns preserved in the War Department's Commissariat Department, and Sixth continuation of the Code of Military Directives [*Svod Voennykh Postanovlenii*], 1846, pg. 100, §§ 175-178 .

(10) Memorandum of the Minister of War to the Commander-in-Chief of the Separate Caucasus Corps, 19 March 1847, No. 1181.

(11) Ditto., 8 March 1849, No. 1090.

(12) Memorandum of the Minister of War to H.I.H. the Commander-in-Chief of the Guards and Grenadier Corps, 7 May 1849, No. 2087.

(13) Order of the Minister of War, 1851, No. 15.

(14) Ditto, 1852, No. 6.

(15) Collection of Laws and Directives, 1827, Book I, pg. 3.

(16) Ibid., 1829, Book III, pg. 27.

(17) Ibid., 1831, Book II, pg. 33.

(18) Sixth continuation of the Code of Military Directives, 1846, pg. 105, §§ 178-180.

(19) Collection of Laws and Directives, 1827, Book I, pg. 3.

(20) Ibid., Book III, pg. 17, and Report of the Host Ataman Colonel Petrov to the Duty General of HIS IMPERIAL MAJESTY's Main Headquarters, 21 September 1827, No. 281.

(21) Information received from the War Department's Commissariat Department.

(22) Ditto.

(23) Collection of Laws and Directives, 1831, Book II, pg. 33.

(24) Information received from the War Department's Commissariat Department, and confirmed patterns preserved there.

(25) Collection of Laws and Directives, 1837, Book III, pg. 47.

(26) Ibid, Book IV, pg. 325.

(27) Ibid., 1838, Book II, pgs. 418-422.

(28) Order of the Minister of War, 1844, No. 1.

(29) Ditto, No. 69, pg 24.

(30) Sixth continuation of the Code of Military Directives, 1846, pgs. 53 and 54, §§ 94-99.

(31) Order of the Minister of War, 1845, No. 66.

(32) Ditto, 1845, No. 72.

(33) Collection of Laws and Directives, 1827, Book I, pg. 3.

(34) Ibid., 1829, Book III, pg. 127.

(35) Confirmed patterns preserved in the War Department's Commissariat Department.

(36) Collection of Laws and Directives, 1837, Book III, pg. 47.

(37) Ibid., Book IV, pg. 325.

(38) Ibid., 1838, Book II, pg. 418, and information received from the War Department's Commissariat Department.

(39) Collection of Laws and Directives, Book II, pg. 283.

(40) Order of the Minister of War, 1844, No. 1.

(41) Sixth continuation of the Code of Military Directives, 1846, pgs. 53, 55, and 56; §§ 94-99.

(42) Order of the Minister of War, 1845, No. 72.

(43) Ditto, 1852, No. 75.

(44) Collection of Laws and Directives, 1827, Book I, pg. 3

(45) Ibid., 1829, Book III, pg. 127.

(46) Confirmed patterns preserved in the War Department's Commissariat Department.

(47) Collection of Laws and Directives, 1831, Book II, pg. 33.

(48) Ibid., 1837, Book III, pg. 47.

(49) Ibid., Book IV, pg. 325.

(50) Ibid., 1838, Book II, pgs. 418-422.

(51) Order of the Minister of War, 1844, No. 1.

(52) Ditto., No. 69, pg. 26.

(53) Ditto., 1845, No. 66.

(54) Ditto., No. 72.

(55) Collection of Laws and Directives, 1826, Book III, pg. 29.

(56) Ibid., 1827, Book I, pg. 3

(57) [No note cited]

(58) Ibid., 1829, Book III. pg. 127.

(59) Ibid., 1837, Book III, pg. 3.

(60) Ibid., pg. 47.

(61) Ibid., Book IV, pg. 325.

(62) Ibid., 1838, Book II, pgs. 413-422.

(63) Order of the Minister of War, 1844, No. 1.

(64) Ditto, 1844, No. 69, pg. 12.

(65) Ditto, 1845, No. 66.

(66) Ditto, 1845, No. 72.

(67) Memorandum of the Minister of War to His Imperial Highness the Commander-in-Chief of the Guards and Grenadier Corps, 27 February 1847, No. 1728.

(68) Order of the Minister or War, 1848, No. 16.

(69) Ditto, 1848, No. 27.

(70) Ditto, 1851, No. 6.

(71) Ditto, 1852, No. 49.

(72) Collection of Laws and Directives, 1827, No. 1, pg. 3.

(73) Ibid., 1829, Book III. pg. 127.

(74) Confirmed patterns preserved in the War Department's Commissariat Department.

(75) Collection of Laws and Directives, 1831, Book II, pg. 33.

(76) Ibid., 1834, Book I, pg. 549.

(77) HIGHEST confirmed Regulation for the First Orenburg Cossack Regiment, 21 March 1835, pgs. 23 and 24.

(78) Ibid., 1837, Book III, pg. 47.

(79) Ibid., Book IV., 325.

(78) Collection of Laws and Directives, 1837, Book III, pg. 47.

(79) Ditto, 1837, Book IV, pg. 325.

(80) Ditto, 1838, Book II, pgs. 418-422, and Second continuation of the Code of Military Directives, 1841, pg. 579, § 197.

(81) Second continuation of the Code of Military Directives, 1841, pg. 56, § 30, pg. 79, § 197.

(82) Order of the head of the War Ministry, 13 April 1842, No. 32.

(83) Memorandum of the Minister of War to the Commander of the Separate Orenburg Corps, 12 October 1843, No. 1216.

(84) Ditto, 20 October 1843, No. 1331.

(85) Order of the Minister of War, 1844, No. 1.

(86) Memorandum of the Minister of War to the Commander of the Separate Orenburg Corps, 7 January 1844, No. 87.

(87) Order of the Minister of War, 1844, No. 69, pg. 26.

(88) Ditto, 1845, No. 66.

(89) Ditto, 1845, No. 72.

(90) Memorandum of the Minister of War to the Commander of the Separate Orenburg Corps, 26 October 1854, No. 1825.

(91) Collection of Laws and Directives, 1827, Book I, pg. 3.

(92) Ibid., 1829, Book III, pg. 127.

(93) Confirmed patterns preserved in the War Department's Commissariat Department.

(94) Collection of Laws and Directives, 1837, Book III, pg. 47.

(95) Ibid., 1837, Book IV, pg. 325.

(96) Ibid., 1838, Book II, pgs. 418-422.

(97) Ibid., 1839, Book III, pg. 5.

(98) Order of the Minister of War, 1845, No. 72, and Third continuation of the Code of Military Directives, 1843, pg. 254, § 5, and pgs. 260 and 261.

(99) Order of the Minister of War, 1844, No. 1.

(100) Ditto, 1845, No. 66.

(101) Ditto, 1845, No. 72.

(102) Memorandum of the Minister of War to the Commander of the Separate Orenburg Corps, 5 April 1849, No. 1484.

(103) Order of the Minister of War, 1852, No. 75.

(104) Collection of Laws and Directives, 1827, Book I, pg. 3.

(105) Ibid., 1827, Book III, pg. 17.

(106) Ibid., 1831, Book II, pg. 139; information received from the War Department's Commissariat Department, and confirmed patterns preserved there.

(107) Collection of Laws and Directives, 1827, Book I, pg. 3.

(108) Ibid., 1827, Book III, pg. 17.

(109) Information received from the War Department's Commissariat Department, and confirmed patterns preserved there

(110) Collection of Laws and Directives, 1832, Book I, pg. 13.

(111) Ibid., 1837, Book III, pg. 47.

(112) Ibid., 1837, Book IV, pg. 325.

(113) Ibid., 1838, Book II, pg. 418-422.

(114) Confirmed patterns preserved in the War Department's Commissariat Department, and a description of confirmed patterns forwarded to the commander of the Separate Orenburg Corps with correspondence from the Duty General of HIS IMPERIAL MAJESTY's Main Headquarters, 2 October 1829, No. 7466.

(115) Collection of Laws and Directives, 1837, Book III, pg. 47.

(116) Ibid., 1837, Book IV, pg. 325.

(117) Information received from the Department of Military Settlements, 8 November 1854, No. 1908, and information received from the acting commander of the Separate Orenburg Corps, 11 March 1848, No. 434.

(118) Order of the Minister of War, 1844, No. 1.

(119) Ditto, 1844, No. 69.

(120) Ditto, 1845, No. 72, and information received from the War Department's Commissariat Department.

(121) Memorandum of the Minister of War to the commander of the Separate Orenburg Corps, 12 February 1846, No. 682.

(122) Collection of Laws and Directives, 1827, Book I, pg. 3.

(123) Ibid., 1829, Book III, pg. 127, and information received from the War Department's Commissariat Department.

(124) Information received from the War Department's Commissariat Department.

(125) Collection of Laws and Directives, 1831, Book II, pg. 33.

(126) Ibid., 1837, Book I, pg. 61.

(127) Ibid., 1837, Book III, pg. 47.

(128) Ibid., 1837, Book IV, pg. 325.

(129) Ibid., 1838, Book II, pg. 422.

(130) Memorandum of the director of the Department of Military Settlements to the War Ministry's Commissariat Department, 4 December 1840, No. 3428.

(131) Order of the Minister of War, 1844, No. 1.

(132) Ditto, 1844, No. 69, pg. 26.

(133) Ditto, 1845, No. 66.

(134) Ditto, 1845, No. 72.

(135) Administrative Regulation for the Siberian Line Cossack Host, confirmed 5 December 1846.

(136) Order of the Minister of War, 1851, No. 46.

(137) Ditto, 1851, No. 127.

(138) Collection of Laws and Directives, 1827, Book I, pg. 3.

(139) Ibid., 1829, Book III, pg. 127.

(140) Confirmed patterns preserved in the War Department's Commissariat Department.

(141) Collection of Laws and Directives, 1837, Book III, pg. 47.

(142) Ibid., 1837, Book IV, pg. 325.

(143) Ibid., 1838, Book II, pg. pgs. 418-422.

(144) Ibid., 1839, Book III, pg. 5.

(145) Order of the Minister of War, 1844, No. 1.

(146) Ditto, 1845, No. 66.

(147) Ditto, 1845, No. 72.

(148) Administrative Regulation [Polozhenie] for the Siberian Line Cossack Host, confirmed 5 December 1846.

(149) Information received from the War Department's Commissariat Department, and confirmed patterns preserved there.

(150) [No note cited.]

(151) Collection of Laws and Directives, 1837, Book IV, pg. 325.

(152) Memorandum of the director of the Department of Military Settlements to the War Ministry's Commissariat Department, 22 August 1840, No. 2442.

(153) Memorandum of the director of the Department of Military Settlements to the governor-general of Eastern Siberia, 18 Febru-

ary 1842, No. 512.

(154) Order of the Minister of War, 1844, No. 1.

(155) Administrative Regulation for the Tobolsk Cossack Foot Battalion and Tobolsk Horse Regiment, confirmed 21 October 1849.

(156) Memorandum of the Minister of War to the governor-general of Eastern Siberia and commander of troops stationed there, 31 January 1851, No. 277, and Administrative Regulation for the Irkutsk and Yeniseisk Cossack Regiments, confirmed 4 January 1851.

(157) Administrative Regulation for the Trans-Baikal Cossack Host, confirmed 17 March 1851

(158) Administrative Regulation for foot battalions of the Trans-Baikal Cossack Host, confirmed 21 June [sic - M.C.] 1851.

(159) Order of the Minister of War, 1852, No. 31.

(160) Ditto, 1853, No. 60.

(161) Ditto, 1854, No. 3.

(162) Ditto, 1854, No. 35.

РИСУНКИ

ОДЕЖДЫ и ВООРУЖЕНІЯ

РОССІЙСКИХЪ

ВОЙСКЪ

1825-1855·

# PLATES LIST OF ILLUSTRATIONS

1241. Mounted Cossack. Orenburg Cossack Host, on internal service, 1843-1845.

1242. Foot Cossack. Orenburg Cossack Host, on internal service, 1843-1855.

1243. Field-Grade Officer. Noncombatant Company of the Ufa Cossack Regiment, 1844-1845.

1244. Non-Commissioned Officer. Orenburg Cossack Host, 1845-1855.

1245. Field-Grade Officer and Cossack. Foot Battalions of the Orenburg Cossack Host, 1854-1855.

1246. Cossack. Orenburg Cossack Artillery, 1829-1838.

1247. Non-Commissioned Officer. Teptyar Cossack Regiments, 1829-1835.

1248. Field-Grade Officer. Teptyar Cossack Regiments, 1829-1835.

1249. Cossack. Stavropol Kalmuck Host, 1829-1838.

1250. Company-Grade Officer. Stavropol Kalmuck Host, 1829-1832.

1251. Field-Grade Officer. Stavropol Kalmuck Host, 1832-1838.

1252. Non-Commissioned Officer. Stavropol Kalmuck Host, 1838-1842.

1253. Cossack. Bashkir Cantons, 1829-1838.

1254. Non-Commissioned Officer. Bashkir Cantons, 1829-1838.

1255. Company-Grade Officer. Bashkir Cantons, 1829-1838.

1256. Non-Commissioned Officer. Meshcheryak Cantons, 1829-1838.

1257. Company-Grade Officer. Meshcheryak Cantons, 1829-1838.

1258. Non-Commissioned Officer and Field-Grade Officer. Bashkir Cantons, 1838-1845.

1259. Cossack. Meshcheryak Cantons, 1838-1845.

1260. Company-Grade Officer. Bashkir Cantons, 1845-1855.

1261. Company-Grade Officer and Cossack. Meshcheryak Cantons, 1845-1855.

1262. Cossack and Non-Commissioned Officer. Siberian Line Cossack Host, 1829-1838.

1263. Company-Grade Officer. Siberian Line Cossack Host, 1829-1838.

1264. Cossack and Field-Grade Officer. Siberian Line Cossack Host, 1838-1840.

1265. Field-Grade Officer and Non-Commissioned Officer. Siberian Line Cossack Host, 1840-1845.

1266. Cossack. Siberian Line Cossack Host, 1845-1855.

1267. Field-Grade Officer. Siberian Line Cossack Host, 1845-1855.

1268. Non-Commissioned Officer. Siberian Line Cossack Artillery, 1829-1838.

1269. Non-Commissioned Officer and Cossack. Siberian Town Cossacks and Border Troops, 1829-1853.

1270. Cossack. Siberian Town Cossacks and Border Troops, 1829-1853.

1271. Field-Grade Officer. Siberian Town Cossacks and Border Troops, 1829-1853.

*Cossacks. Terek Family and Khoper Cassack Regiments, 1831-1834*

*Non-commissioned Officers. Mountaineer and Grebensk Cossack Regiments. 1831-1834*

*Company-Grade Officers. Kuban and Volga Cossack Regiments, 1831-1834*

*Field-Grade Officers. Mozdok and Kizlyar-Terek Cossack Regiments, 1831-1834*

*Cossacks. Caucasian and Kuban Cossack Regiments, 1834-1845*

*Non-Commissioned Officers. Stavropol and Khoper Cossack Regiments. 1834-1845*

*Company-Grade Officers. Volga and Mountaineer Cossack Regiments, 1834-1845*

*Field-Grade Officers. Mozdok and Grebensk Cossack Regiments, 1834-1845*

*Cossack, Terek Cossack Regiment, and Company-Grade Officers, Kizlyar Cossack Regiment. 1834-1836*

*Field-Grade Officer. Stavropol Cossack Regiment. 1843-1845*

*Cossack, Laba Cossack Regiment, and Non-Commissioned Officer, Vladikavkaz Cossack Regiment. 1843-1845*

*Cossacks. Caucasian Cossack Regiments, 1845-1855*

*Field-Grade Officers. Kuban and Laba Cossack Regiment, 1845-1855*

*Non-Commissioned Officers. Stavropol and Khoper Cossack Regiments, 1845-1855*

*Cossacks. Volga and Mountain Cossack Regiments. 1845-1855*

*Company-Grade Officers. Mozdok and Grebensk Cossack Regiments, 1845-1855*

*Company-Grade Officer, Vladikavkaz Cossack Regiment, and Cossack, Kizlyar Family Cossack Regiment, 1845-1855*

*Cossack. 1st Sunzha Cossack Regiment, 1847-1855*

*Company-Grade Officer and Cossack. 1st Caucasian Cossack Foot Battalion, 1849-1855*

*Company-Grade Officer and Horseman, Daghestan Irregular Horse Regiment, 1851-1855*

*Cossack. Artillery of the Caucasian Line Cossack Host, 1845-1855*

*Company-Grade Officer and Non-Commissioned Officer. Artillery of the Caucasian Cossack Line, 1845-1855*

*Non-Commissioned Officer. Astrakhan Cossack Hosts, 1829-1838*

*Company-Grade Officer. Astrakhan Cossack Host, 1829-1838*

*Non-Commissioned Officer and Cossack. Astrakhan Cossack Host, 1838-1845*

*Field-grade Officer. Astrakhan Cossack Host, 1838-1845*

*Cossack. Astrakhan Cossack Host, 1845-1855*

*Company-Grade Officer. Astrakhan Cossack Host, 1845-1855*

*Cossack. Astrakhan Cossack Artillery, 1829-1838*

*Non-commissioned Officer. Astrakhan Cossack Artillery, 1838-1845*

*Cossack. Ural Cossack Host, 1829-1838*

*Field-grade Officer. Ural Cossack Host, 1829-1838*

*Non-Commissioned Officer. Ural Cossack Host, 1838-1845*

*Company-Grade Officer. Ural Cossack Host, 1845-1855*

*Cossack. Leib-Ural Cossack Sotnia, 1826-1828*

*Company-Grade Officer. Leib-Ural Cossack Sotnia, 1826-1829*

*Non-Commissioned Officer. Leib-Ural Cossack Sotnia, 1828-1838*

*Private. L.-Gds. Ural Cossack Sotnia, 1838-1845*

*Field-grade Officer. L.-Gds. Ural Cossack Sotnia, 1838-1845*

*Non-Commissioned Officer. rivate. L.-Gds. Ural Cossack Sotnia, 1845-1855*

*Field-grade Officer and Private. L.-Gds. Ural Cossack Double-Squadron, 1848-1855*

*Cossack and Field-Grade Officer. Orenburg Cossack Host, 1829-1838*

*Cossack. 1st Orenburg Cossack Regiment, 1835-1838*

*Company-Grade Officer. 1st Orenburg Cossack Regiment, 1835-1838*

*Noncombatant. 1st Orenburg Cossack Regiment, 1835-1842*

*Company-Grade Officer. Orenburg Cossack Host, 1838-1840*

*Cossack. 1st Orenburg Cossack Regiment, 1838-1845*

*Mounted Cossack. Orenburg Cossack Host, on internal service, 1843-1845*

*Foot Cossack. Orenburg Cossack Host, on internal service, 1843-1855*

*Field-Grade Officer. Noncombatant Company of the Ufa Cossack Regiment, 1844-1845*

*Non-Commissioned Officer. Orenburg Cossack Host, 1845-1855*

*Field-Grade Officer and Cossack. Foot Battalions of the Orenburg Cossack Host, 1854-1855*

*Cossack. Orenburg Cossack Artillery, 1829-1838*

*Non-Commissioned Officer. Teptyar Cossack Regiments, 1829-1835*

*Field-Grade Officer. Teptyar Cossack Regiments, 1829-1835*

*Cossack. Stavropol Kalmuck Host, 1829-1838*

*Company-Grade Officer. Stavropol Kalmuck Host, 1829-1832*

*Field-Grade Officer. Stavropol Kalmuck Host, 1832-1838*

1252

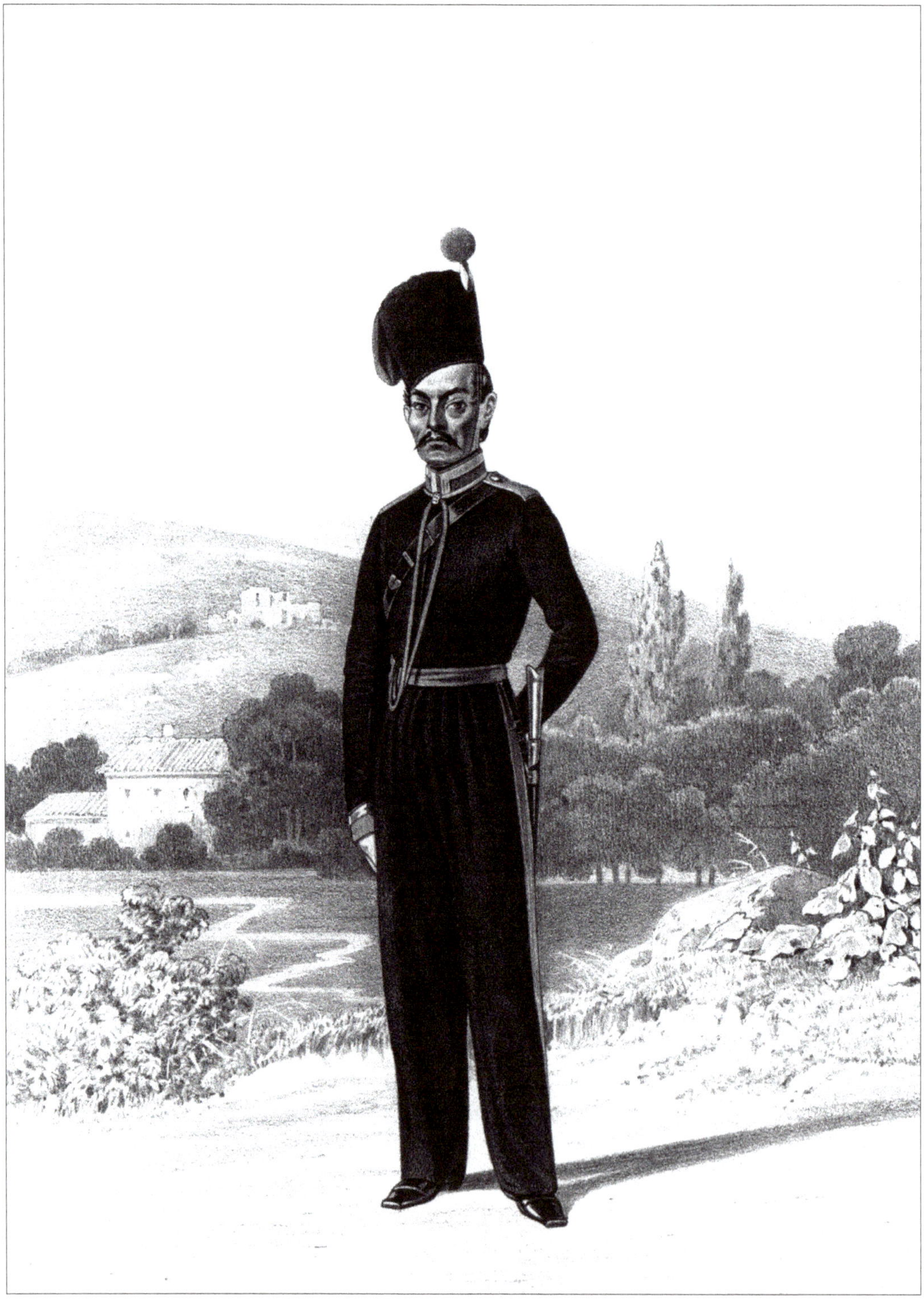

*Non-Commissioned Officer. Stavropol Kalmuck Host, 1838-1842*

1253

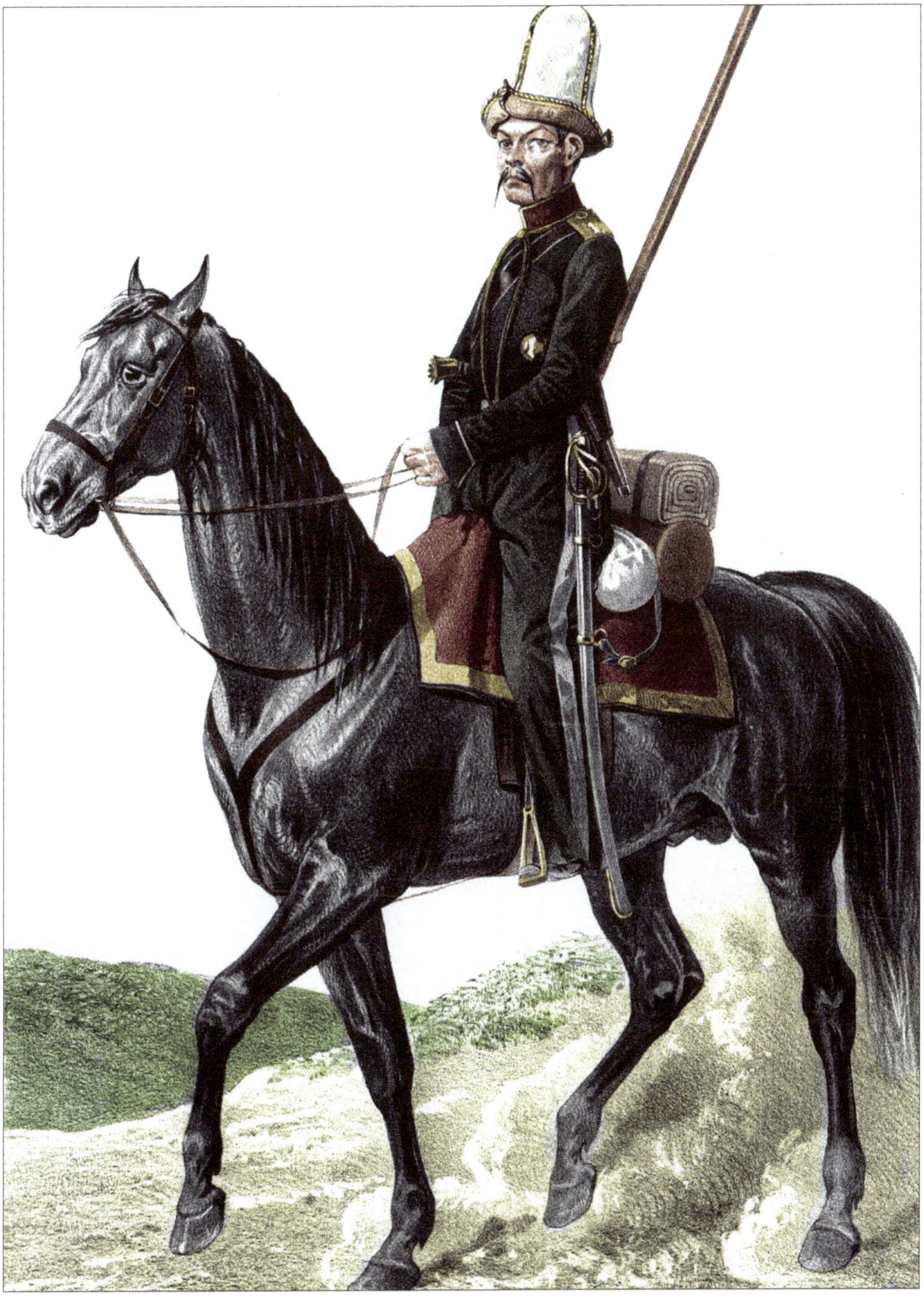

*Cossack. Bashkir Cantons, 1829-1838*

*Non-Commissioned Officer. Bashkir Cantons, 1829-1838*

*Company-Grade Officer. Bashkir Cantons, 1829-1838*

1256

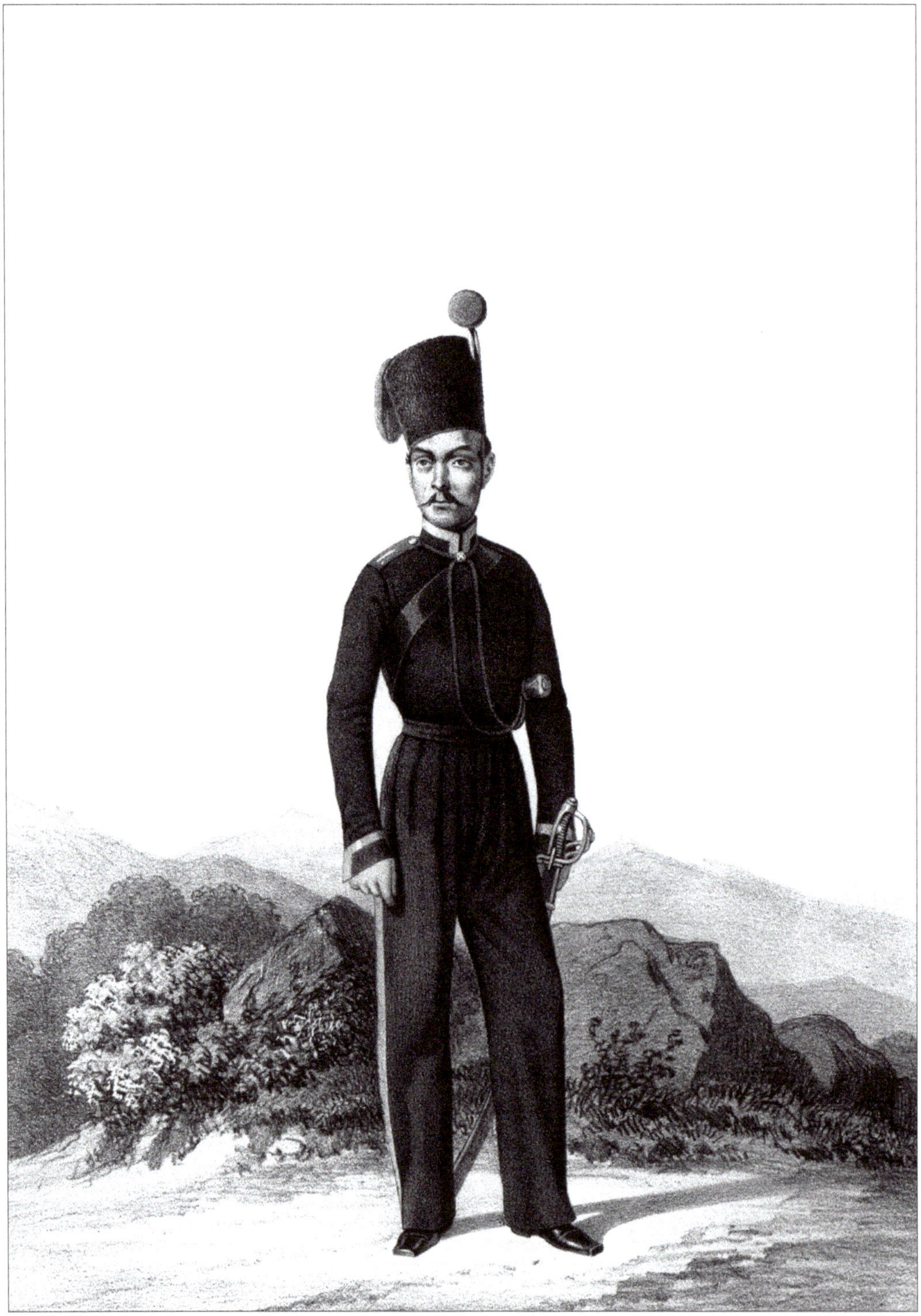

*Non-Commissioned Officer. Meshcheryak Cantons, 1829-1838*

*Company-Grade Officer. Meshcheryak Cantons, 1829-1838*

*Non-Commissioned Officer and Field-Grade Officer. Bashkir Cantons, 1838-1845*

*Cossack. Meshcheryak Cantons, 1838-1845*

*Company-Grade Officer. Bashkir Cantons, 1845-1855*

*Company-Grade Officer and Cossack. Meshcheryak Cantons, 1845-1855*

*Cossack and Non-Commissioned Officer. Siberian Line Cossack Host, 1829-1838*

*Company-Grade Officer. Siberian Line Cossack Host, 1829-1838*

*Cossack and Field-Grade Officer. Siberian Line Cossack Host, 1838-1840*

*Field-Grade Officer and Non-Commissioned Officer. Siberian Line Cossack Host, 1840-1845*

*Cossack. Siberian Line Cossack Host, 1845-1855*

*Field-Grade Officer. Siberian Line Cossack Host, 1845-1855*

*Non-Commissioned Officer. Siberian Line Cossack Artillery, 1829-1838*

*Non-Commissioned Officer and Cossack. Siberian Town Cossacks and Border Troops, 1829-1853*

*Cossack. Siberian Town Cossacks and Border Troops, 1829-1853*

*Field-Grade Officer. Siberian Town Cossacks and Border Troops, 1829-1853*

# SOLDIERS, WEAPONS & UNIFORMS ALREADY PUBLISHED
## (SOME TITLES)

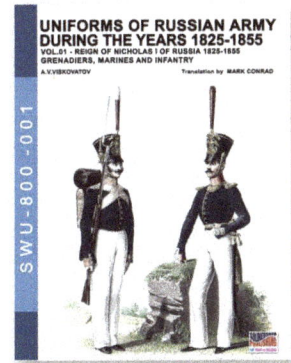
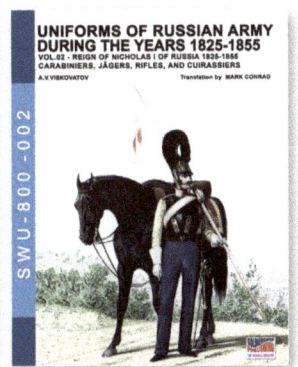
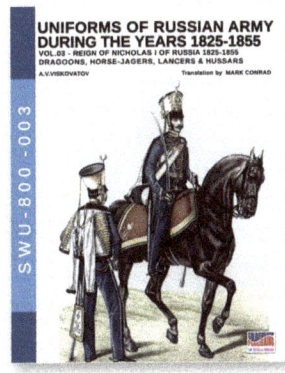
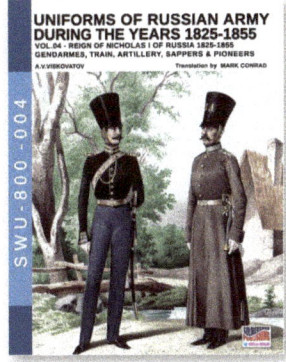

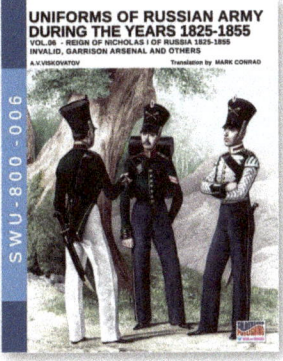

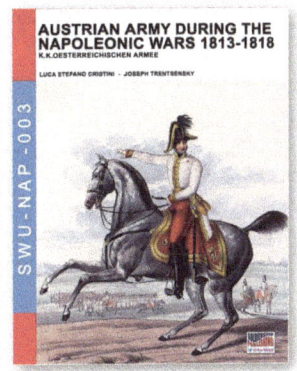
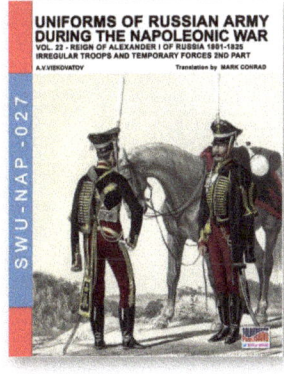

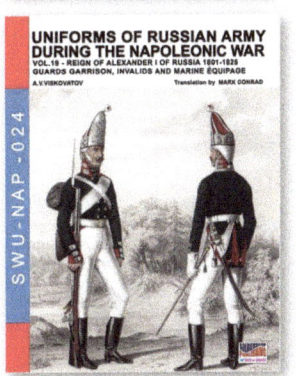